The World from Beginnings to 4000 BCE

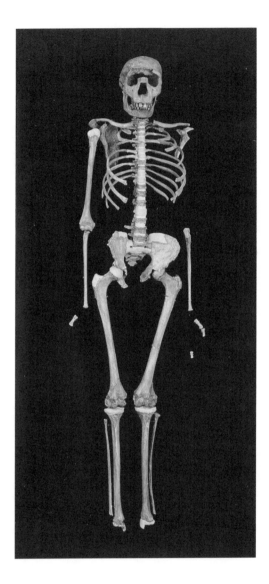

The
New
Oxford
World
History

The World
from Beginnings
to 4000 BCE

Ian Tattersall

OXFORD

UNIVERSITY PRESS

2008

OXFORD

UNIVERSITY PRESS

Oxford University Press, Inc., publishes works that further
Oxford University's objective of excellence
in research, scholarship, and education.

Oxford   New York
Auckland   Cape Town   Dar es Salaam   Hong Kong   Karachi
Kuala Lumpur   Madrid   Melbourne   Mexico City   Nairobi
New Delhi   Shanghai   Taipei   Toronto

With offices in
Argentina   Austria   Brazil   Chile   Czech Republic   France   Greece
Guatemala   Hungary   Italy   Japan   Poland   Portugal   Singapore
South Korea   Switzerland   Thailand   Turkey   Ukraine   Vietnam

Copyright © 2008 by Ian Tattersall

Published by Oxford University Press, Inc.
198 Madison Avenue, New York, New York 10016

www.oup.com

Oxford is a registered trademark of Oxford University Press

Design: Alexis Siroc
Logo design: Nora Wertz

Library of Congress Cataloging-in-Publication Data
Tattersall, Ian.
The world from beginnings to 4000 BCE / Ian Tattersall.
p. cm.
Includes bibliographical references and index.
ISBN 978-0-19-516712-2; 978-0-19-533315-2 (pbk.)
1. Human evolution.   2. Fossil hominids.   I. Title.
GN281.T375 2007
599.93'8—dc22   2007025714

1 3 5 7 9 8 6 4 2

Printed in the United States of America
on acid-free paper

Frontispiece: *The skeleton of the "Turkana Boy" (from 1.6 million years ago), who would have topped six feet in maturity.* Photo by Denis Finnin, courtesy American Museum of Natural History.

Contents

Editors' Preface

Roughly 1.6 million years ago, Turkana Boy strode through the savanna of what today is northern Kenya. He was tall and long-legged and walked dozens of miles a day. He had lost most of the hair that had once covered early hominids and looked impressively human, yet Turkana Boy could not talk. The species *Homo ergaster*, of which Turkana Boy was a member, was a walking, but not yet talking, type of human that would eventually be replaced. One of several hominid species that predated our own *Homo sapiens, Homo ergaster* had many talents and abilities, skillfully wielding stone tools to perform increasingly complex tasks and, notably, inventing the handaxe.

The history of ancient bipeds and early humans reveals how each particular species, including *Homo ergaster,* faced challenges ranging from climate change to problems at the chromosomal level. These early humans had varying capacities and levels of intelligence, eventually changing from beings with massive teeth, protruding jaws, hairy bodies, and small brains to a species more like us. Some species succeeded, others became extinct, and along the way, new species appeared, sometimes intermingling with older ones. Humans became different and even brainier in processes that occurred in many parts of the world. The development of early humans from 5 million to 7000 BCE still has many unknowns, but from bones and artifacts that have been found around the world, anthropologists and archaeologists have been able to recreate some of the drama of human evolution. They can now effectively demonstrate the ways in which one species of humans replaced another, finally producing our own version of humanity.

This book is part of the New Oxford World History, an innovative series that offers readers an informed, lively, and up-to-date history of the world and its people that represents a significant change from the "old" world history. Only a few years ago, world history generally amounted to a history of the West—Europe and the United States—with small amounts of information from the rest of the world. Some versions of the old world history drew attention to every part of the world *ex-*

cept Europe and the United States. Readers of that kind of world history could get the impression that somehow the rest of the world was made up of exotic people who had strange customs and spoke difficult languages. Still another kind of "old" world history presented the story of areas or peoples of the world by focusing primarily on the achievements of great civilizations. One learned of great buildings, influential world religions, and mighty rulers but little of ordinary people or more general economic and social patterns. Interactions among the world's peoples were often told from only one perspective.

This series tells world history differently. First, it is comprehensive, covering all countries and regions of the world and investigating the total human experience—even those of so-called peoples without histories living far from the great civilizations. "New" world historians thus have in common an interest in all of human history, even going back millions of years before there were written human records. A few "new" world histories even extend their focus to the entire universe, a "big history" perspective that dramatically shifts the beginning of the story back to the Big Bang. Some see the "new" global framework of world history today as viewing the world from the vantage point of the moon, as one scholar put it. We agree. But we also want to take a close-up view, analyzing and reconstructing the significant experiences of all of humanity.

This is not to say that everything that has happened everywhere and in all time periods can be recovered or is worth knowing, but there is much to be gained by considering both the separate and interrelated stories of different societies and cultures. Making these connections is still another crucial ingredient of the "new" world history. It emphasizes connectedness and interactions of all kinds—cultural, economic, political, religious, and social—involving peoples, places, and processes. It makes comparisons and finds similarities. Emphasizing both the comparisons and interactions is critical to developing a global framework that can deepen and broaden historical understanding, whether the focus is on a specific country or region or on the whole world.

The rise of the new world history as a discipline comes at an opportune time. The interest in world history in schools and among the general public is vast. We travel to one another's nations, converse and work with people around the world, and are changed by global events. War and peace affect populations worldwide as do economic conditions and the state of our environment, communications, and health and medicine. The New Oxford World History presents local histories in a global context and gives an overview of world events seen through the eyes of ordinary people. This combination of the local and the global further defines the new world history. Understanding the workings of global and local conditions in the past gives us tools for examining our own world and for envisioning the interconnected future that is in the making.

Bonnie G. Smith
Anand Yang

The World
from Beginnings
to 4000 BCE

CHAPTER I

Evolutionary Processes

It is impossible for human beings fully to understand either themselves or their long prehuman history without knowing something of the process (or, rather, processes) by which our remarkable species became what it is. This is, as (almost) everybody knows, evolution. And although most of us have a vague idea of what evolution is all about, few realize quite how many factors have typically been involved in the evolutionary histories that gave rise to the diversity of today's living world. For evolution is not, as we often believe, a simple, linear process; rather, it is an untidy affair involving many different causes and influences.

Evolutionary biology is a branch of science, and our perception of the nature of science itself is often flawed. Many of us look upon science as a rather absolutist system of belief. We have a vague notion that science strives to "prove" the correctness of this or that idea about nature and that scientists are aloof paragons of objectivity in white coats. But the idea that some beliefs are "scientifically proven" is in many ways an oxymoron. In reality, science does not actually set out to provide positive proof of anything. Rather, it is a constantly self-correcting means of understanding the world and the universe around us. To put it in a nutshell, the vital characteristic of any scientific idea is not that it can be proven to be true but that it can, at least potentially, be shown to be *false* (which is not the case for all kinds of proposition).

Science has made huge strides in the last three centuries or so, bringing humankind extraordinary material benefits. And it has advanced not only through a remarkable series of insights into how nature works but by the testing of those insights—or of aspects of them—and the rejection of those that ultimately cannot stand up to scrutiny. Science is thus inherently a system of provisional, rather than absolute, knowledge. Unlike religious knowledge, which is based on faith, scientific knowledge is grounded in doubt—which is why these two kinds of knowing are complementary rather than conflicting. Science and religion deal with two intrinsically different kinds of knowledge and address equally important but utterly different needs of the human psyche.

Clearly, then, to say disparagingly that "evolution is *only* a theory" is to dismiss the entire basis of the very science to which our unprecedented modern living standards and longevities owe so much. For evolution is a theory that is as well supported as any other theory in science. At the same time, though, it is a theory that is widely misunderstood. A common misperception of evolution is that it is a simple matter of change over time: a story of almost inexorable improvement over the ages, in which time and change are pretty much synonymous. But the real story is a lot more complicated—and a lot more interesting—than that.

In 1859, when the English naturalist Charles Darwin's revolutionary book *On the Origin of Species by Natural Selection* was published, the notion of evolution was already in the air. Geologists and antiquarians were aware that both Earth and humankind had much longer histories than the 6,000 years derived from counting "begats" in the Old Testament; and as early as 1809, the French naturalist Jean-Baptiste de Lamarck had already discarded the notion of the fixed and unchanging nature of living species in favor of a view of the history of life that involved ancestral species giving rise to newer and different ones. Lamarck's insight derived from careful studies of the fossils of mollusks, which he found he could arrange into series over time, one species gradually giving way to another. But Lamarck was even more daring than this. In an age when belief in the literal truth of the Bible reigned supreme, he was even willing to speculate that humans had arisen through a similar process, from apelike forerunners that had adopted upright posture.

These were brilliant perceptions, but Lamarck was too far ahead of his time for his insight to be appreciated by his contemporaries. What's more, history has also treated him harshly, this time because of his explanation of how one species could transform into another. Lamarck believed that species had to be in harmony with their environments, yet from his paleontological studies he knew that environments were unstable over time. So species had to be able to change too. And this, Lamarck thought, must have been achieved through changes in their behaviors. Like many others of his time Lamarck believed that, during the lifetime of each individual, such new behaviors would elicit changes in its structure, and that these changes would be passed along from parent to offspring. It was such a process, he thought, that had given rise to the pattern of change he saw in the fossil record.

Most of Lamarck's colleagues savagely (and justifiably) attacked this notion of the inheritance of acquired characteristics, with the result that the evolution baby was thrown out with the bathwater of a flawed mechanism of change. Yet Lamarck had dramatically opened a door that could never again be fully closed. Indeed, even before Lamarck went public with his ideas, the polymath Erasmus Darwin (Charles Darwin's grandfather) had published a work that anticipated some elements of his grandson's thinking, although they did not include the key idea of natural selection. And as early as 1844 the Scottish encyclopedist Robert Chambers argued (anonymously) that all species had developed according to natural laws, without recourse to a divine creator. By the time the 1850s rolled around, then, Western intellectuals were subliminally prepared for an explicit statement that all life forms had evolved from an ancient common ancestor.

Charles Darwin nurtured such a notion for two decades, more or less ever since returning in 1836 from a five-year round-the-world voyage (1831–36) on the British Navy brigantine *Beagle*. He was, however, reluctant to publish his ideas about evolution in a climate of opinion that was still dominated by biblical beliefs regarding the origins of the Earth and living things. It thus came as a shock to him when in 1858 he received from his younger contemporary Alfred Russel Wallace a manuscript entitled *On the Tendency of Varieties to Depart Indefinitely from the Original Type*, with a request for help in getting it published.

Wallace was an impoverished naturalist who made his living by collecting animal and plant specimens in exotic and uncomfortable places, and the ideas expressed in his manuscript had come to him during a bout of malarial fever endured on the remote Indonesian island of Ternate. These ideas were for all intents and purposes identical to those that had been maturing in Darwin's mind for years. So who had priority on the notion of evolution? The moral dilemma was resolved by the simultaneous presentation to London's Linnaean Society, in July 1858, of Wallace's paper and of some older drafts written by Darwin. Darwin then began writing night and day; his great book was published a year later, and it sealed his popular identification with evolution by natural selection.

The central notion of both Wallace's and Darwin's contributions was that the diversity of life in the world today and in the past, and the pattern of resemblances among those life forms, are the results of branching descent from a single common ancestor. "Descent with modification" was Darwin's succinct summary of the evolutionary process. And thus stated it is, indeed, the only explanation of the diversity of life that actually predicts what we observe in nature. It has never been validly disputed on scientific grounds (and only people with religious motivations have ever claimed to do so). Virtually all the subsequent vociferous scientific argument on the subject of evolution has been over its mechanisms, not over its power to explain what we see in the living world around us. Mechanisms, however, remain a vexing question.

Both Darwin and Wallace were highly experienced and perceptive observers of nature, fully appreciating the complexity of the interactions that occur among living organisms. And to both of them, natural selection (Darwin's term) was the central evolutionary process. This is how it works. As both naturalists noted, every species consists of individuals that vary slightly among themselves. What is more, in each generation far more individuals are born than survive to reach maturity and reproduce. Those that succeed are the ones that are "fittest" in terms of the characteristics that ensure their survival and successful reproduction. If such characteristics are inherited, which most are, then the features that ensure greater fitness will be disproportionately represented in each succeeding generation, as the less fit lose out in the competition to reproduce. In this way, the appearance of every species will change over time, as each becomes better "adapted" to the environmental conditions in which the fitter individuals reproduce more successfully. Natural selection is thus no more than the combination of any and all factors in the environment that contribute to the differential reproductive success of individuals.

If you think about it a little, natural selection seems a logical inevitability as long as more individuals are born than survive and reproduce—which is always true. And there is thus no doubt that a process of natural sorting is continually happening within populations—even where it tends to trim away the extreme variations, rather than to move the average type in one direction or another. Nonetheless, in Victorian England it took natural selection a long time to catch on as an explanation of evolutionary change. In contrast, the idea that our species, *Homo sapiens,* is related by descent to "lower" forms of life became quite rapidly accepted—after an initial reaction of public shock and horror immortalized by the reported comment of a bishop's wife: "Descended from an ape? My dear, let us hope it is not true. But if it is, let us pray that it does not become generally known."

Darwin and Wallace came up with their evolutionary formulations in the absence of any accurate idea of how inheritance is controlled. The observation—familiar to animal breeders since the dawn of time—that particular characteristics are passed on from parents to their offspring was enough for their purposes. It was only after the birth of the science of genetics at the turn of the twentieth century that explicit discussion of evolutionary mechanisms really took off; but in fact the first principles of genetics had been discovered as early as 1866 in what is now the Czech Republic by the abbot Gregor Mendel. However, Mendel's article about this, printed in an obscure local publication, made no initial impact. His crucial insight—that inheritance is controlled from generation to generation by independent factors that do not blend—languished until 1900, when it was independently rediscovered by three different groups of scientists.

Before Mendel's time it was generally believed that the parental characteristics of sexually reproducing organisms were somehow combined in their offspring and that it was the blend that was passed on to subsequent generations, between which it was blended again. Mendel saw, in contrast, that physical appearance was controlled by distinct elements—now known as *genes*—that did not lose their identity in the passage between generations. He recognized that each individual of a sexually reproducing species possesses two copies (now known as alleles) of each gene, one inherited from each parent. If one allele is dominant over the other, it will mask the latter's effects in determining the physical characteristics of the offspring. But it has no greater a chance of being passed on to the next generation than its recessive companion has, and each of these factors is preserved independently from generation to generation.

We now know that the development of most physical characteristics is controlled by multiple genes and that a single gene may be involved in determining several characteristics. What's more, we also now know that genes of different types may play very different roles in the developmental process. Mendel was exceedingly lucky in having chosen to study characters of sweet-pea plants that were simply controlled by single genes. Nonetheless, his principle holds: genes retain their identities when passing from one generation to the next—except when errors are made in the replicating process. Once in a while a gene is inaccurately copied from the parental original during the reproductive process. These changes, known as mutations, may have effects of various kinds and magnitudes (and most are decidedly disadvantageous), but they are the source of the new variants that make evolutionary change possible. The molecule of heredity is now known to be deoxyribonucleic acid (DNA).

Once the basic concepts of genetic change had been worked out early in the twentieth century, evolutionary biology buzzed with competing theories for how the evolutionary process proceeded. As you might expect, every possibility was being explored. All scientists agreed that lineages of organisms tended to show physical—and presumably genetic—change over time. But how? Some attributed the change to what they

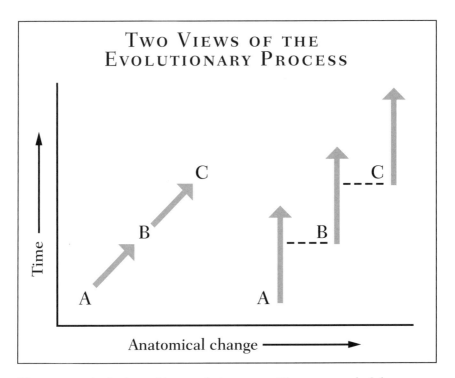

TWO VIEWS OF THE EVOLUTIONARY PROCESS

Time

A

B

C

A

B

C

Anatomical change

There are two basic views of how evolution occurs. The arrows at the left represent the process of "phyletic gradualism," whereby one species gradually transforms over time into another under the guiding hand of natural selection. In contrast, the notion of punctuated equilibria (right) sees change as episodic; species are essentially stable entities that give rise to new species in relatively short-term events. After Ian Tattersall, The Human Odyssey *(1993).*

called mutation pressure—the rate at which mutations occur. Others favored the idea that new species were generated from sports—individuals that showed major changes relative to their parents. Yet another group of biologists argued that organisms had built-in tendencies toward change. Almost everyone was bothered to some extent by the obvious discontinuities that can be observed in nature, but at first only a minority opted for natural selection as the driving force of evolutionary change.

By the 1920s and 1930s a consensus began to emerge from this busy process of exploration, as naturalists, geneticists, and paleontologists converged on a unifying theory of evolution known grandly as the evolutionary synthesis. Exponents of each discipline brought different offerings to the table. The geneticists brought their newfound understanding of the mechanisms by which genes interact in reproducing populations and of how they are passed along and occasionally modified between generations. The naturalists brought their expertise in the diversity of nature and in what species were and how new species might be formed. And the paleontologists brought the history of life: an eloquent demonstration via fossils of the paths along which life had evolved.

The geneticists had the upper hand in this convergence. Although some paleontologists and naturalists had initial misgivings, by midcentury the process of evolution was widely understood as being little more than the slow but inexorable action of natural selection in modifying the gene pools of species over vast spans of time. In this picture, species lost their individuality as they became no more than arbitrarily defined segments of steadily evolving lineages. Of course, the vast diversity of life argued strongly for the splitting of lineages too; but even this was seen as another gradual process that occurred as the "adaptive landscape" shifted beneath species' feet when environments changed in different ways in different regions. Habitat changes and geographical factors such as mountain ranges rising or rivers changing course were seen as forces that divided single parental species into two or more descendant populations, diverting each into its own particular adaptive avenue. Eventually, each population would become different enough from its parent to qualify as a new species. Simple, eh? Too simple, maybe.

The grand edifice of the evolutionary synthesis was elegant in its simplicity, and it had all the appeal that simple elegance exerts. But, as the philosopher Thomas Kuhn gained well-deserved fame for pointing out, science progresses largely by occasionally overturning explanatory paradigms that no longer fit the accumulating facts. It was inevitable, then, that eventually somebody would notice that the synthesis conveniently ignored some of the complexities in nature that were becoming ever more evident. The first effective blow came from the direction of paleontology—the study of **ancient life forms**—a branch of evolutionary science that had taken something of a back seat to genetics in the formulation of the synthesis.

As Charles Darwin had been well aware, the fossil record does not in fact furnish the smooth flow of intermediate forms that would be expected under the notion of gradual evolution that he favored. But in Darwin's day paleontology was in its infancy as a science, and it was still realistic to argue that although the expected intermediates had not yet been discovered, someday they would be. A century and more later, though, during which time untold numbers of fossils had been recovered, sorted, and analyzed, this argument was beginning to wear a bit

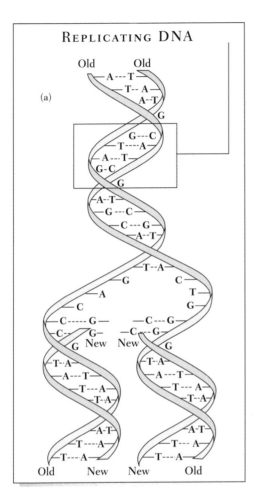

REPLICATING DNA

(a)

Old   Old

Old   New   New   Old

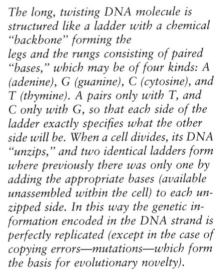

The long, twisting DNA molecule is structured like a ladder with a chemical "backbone" forming the legs and the rungs consisting of paired "bases," which may be of four kinds: A (adenine), G (guanine), C (cytosine), and T (thymine). A pairs only with T, and C only with G, so that each side of the ladder exactly specifies what the other side will be. When a cell divides, its DNA "unzips," and two identical ladders form where previously there was only one by adding the appropriate bases (available unassembled within the cell) to each unzipped side. In this way the genetic information encoded in the DNA strand is perfectly replicated (except in the case of copying errors—mutations—which form the basis for evolutionary novelty).

thin. For the enlarged record still stubbornly refused to yield the expected series of intermediate forms. Instead, as the American paleontologists Niles Eldredge and Stephen Jay Gould argued in a paper published in 1972, the signal emerging from the fossil record was not one of gradual change but one of overall stability with short bursts of change (a pattern they called "punctuated equilibria"). As a rule, they pointed out, fossil species have not generally shown evidence of slow change from one into another over the ages. Rather, they have tended to appear in the record quite suddenly, to persist relatively unchanged for periods of time that could stretch into the millions of years, and then to disappear with equal suddenness, to be replaced by other species, which might or might not have been their close relatives. The gaps in the fossil record, Eldredge and Gould suggested, might not simply reflect a lack of information but, rather, might actually be telling us something. More was going on than simple linear change under the guiding hand of natural selection.

The missing ingredient turns out to be a very complex set of factors. Eldredge and Gould focused on speciation, the means by which a parent species gives rise to one or more descendant species. We only think that gradual evolution occurs, they pointed out, because Darwin told us so, very persuasively. But we *know* that the splitting of lineages (speciation) occurs, for otherwise life could never have diversified—giving us the pattern of groups-within-groups that we see in nature and that is predicted by an evolutionary pattern of ancestry and descent. They saw speciation as a short-term event (maybe, they hazarded, taking 5,000 to 50,000 years—in geological terms, the blink of an eye), rather than one involving gradual change over vast spans of time. They also suggested that most change was concentrated around the event of speciation itself.

The most persuasive evidence for gradual change would appear to be the undeniable indications in the fossil record of long-term evolutionary trends, such as the enlargement of the brain among members of our zoological family, Hominidae (members of Hominidae are hominids), over the past 2 million years or so. Yet, as Eldredge and Gould proposed, evolutionary trends could just as well be explained by competition *among species* as by processes taking place *within species* under natural selection. To take the hominid example, it is quite plausible to attribute the apparently rather steady hominid brain-size enlargement that we see in the fossil record to the relative success of larger-brained hominid species in the competition for life rather than to the competitive advantage of larger-brained individuals within each population. According to Eldredge and Gould's theory, then, each species as a whole plays a part in the evolutionary process, as an actor in the evolutionary play. This idea revolutionized the way in which we perceive evolution.

At this point it's probably necessary to say something about what species are, which is trickier than one might imagine. Back in 1864 the French biologist Pierre Trémaux wrote, "Of definitions of species, there are as many as there are naturalists." Almost a century and a half later his words ring as true as ever. Species are the basic kinds of organisms, the fundamental units into which nature is packaged. Yet there is little agreement on what exactly species are and on how to recognize them. Of course, there are self-evident discontinuities in the living world, and it is generally acknowledged that members of the same species can interbreed successfully, whereas members of different species cannot.

*An example of two closely related (yet distinctively different) species descended
from the same common ancestor. Both are lemurs (lower primates) from
Madagascar:* Propithecus verreauxi *(right) and* Propithecus tattersalli *(left).*
Courtesy of David Haring/Duke University Primate Center.

But when it comes to stating a precise definition, things are not so
simple. Lack of successful interbreeding can be a result of lack of incli-
nation, of incompatibilities of the reproductive apparatus, or of the inability of the progeny to develop or reproduce successfully. Each of these
things expresses itself in a different way and will give rise to a different
species definition. What's more, members of different species tend to
look different or to choose different habitats, and species definitions
have been based on these criteria, too. Defining species becomes even
more difficult when we are dealing with extinct species. For these are
known only from their bones, and they exist in another dimension, time,
that adds its own complexities.

Among mammals such as ourselves, fully individuated new species
(and it is important to realize that each species is, in an sense, an individual entity) are derived from subpopulations of existing species that
for some reason become isolated from the parent populations. If the
isolated groups are small, novel characteristics that might appear within
their number may become incorporated and passed down through gen-

erations. Small group size is apparently a prerequisite for significant evolutionary change of any kind, because large populations are simply too hard to modify. And it is in such populations that physical novelties must thus occur. But physical change itself has nothing itself to do with speciation, which is the development of reproductive isolation—that is, the separation of a new species. Moreover, we cannot even use the concept of "speciation" to help us in reaching a species definition. This is because speciation is not a mechanism but a result, one that may come about for a whole variety of different reasons. Thus, while it is clear that species are fundamental to the evolutionary process, it is also evident that species are to biologists much as pornography is to some U.S. Supreme Court justices, who cannot seem to define it even though they claim to know it when they see it.

The edifice of evolutionary theory is thus very much under construction, and it will continue to be tinkered with as long as there are scientists around to refine it. But despite a plethora of competing viewpoints, it is possible to discern the broad directions in which our understanding of evolution is likely to develop. Most importantly, adding the roles of species and populations to those of individuals in the evolutionary process helps to clarify how change may take place.

When the evolutionary synthesis was formulated, the individual was seen as the paramount entity in evolution. Some individuals were better adapted to prevailing circumstances than others; and it was the reproductive success of the well adapted, and the failure of the poorly adapted, that ultimately propelled populations—over vast periods of time—along the path of improved adaptation. All seemed as simple as that, and this view persuasively reduced complex and critically important phenomena such as the emergence of new species to little more than passive consequences of a basic process of sorting among individuals. Through this process a population could become better adapted to the same environment, it could mark time, or it could change to adapt to a new environment, and that was about all that was needed to make the whole thing work. An attractive formulation for the tidy-minded, perhaps; but, alas, nature turns out to be a rather untidy place.

For a start, let's look at environmental change. Ever since Darwin's day, everyone has agreed that shifting—sometimes dramatically shifting—climates have been marked features of Earth's history and have also been major determinants of the evolutionary patterns we see in the fossil record. Certainly the period during which the human family, Hominidae, has been around has witnessed huge oscillations in environmental circumstances all over the globe. For instance, as recently as 20,000 years ago, parts of Europe that today are covered by oak forests lay under ice sheets a quarter-mile thick. But as this example suggests, such changes have tended to take place on relatively short time scales, much shorter than those that would be necessary for gradual transformation of species, generation by generation, under natural selection. And even in cases where adaptation to dramatically new environments might theoretically be possible, there are more plausible outcomes than adaptive change on the spot. For if a population is suddenly affected by major habitat change, migration to more congenial circumstances, or local or even total extinction, are much more likely to occur than is slow generation-by-generation change to another adaptive state—by which time circumstances might well have changed again.

And let's look at adaptation, too. Adaptation is a process whereby members of a species fit into their environments in such a way that they can survive and flourish. Too often, though, we look upon adaptation as something that involves the optimization of particular features. We see it as a business of maximally improving the organism's fit with its environment in every characteristic. Yet a moment's thought should be enough to show that this cannot be the case. The process that governs adaptation within populations is natural selection, which operates by promoting or suppressing the reproductive success of individuals. Whole individuals, not their separate features. And every individual is an enormously complicated bundle of characteristics, most of which are controlled by many genes and are in turn linked genetically to other characters. There is, in short, no way in which the evolutionary fate of a particular characteristic can be determined without affecting the destinies of many other attributes as well.

Each organism succeeds or fails as the sum of its parts. And as far as the population is concerned, there is no way for particular characteristics to be singled out for promotion or elimination—although with enough imagination it is certainly possible to dream up situations in which a particular attribute might be crucial to success or failure, particularly among features directly related to reproduction. Yet we tend very easily to talk about the "evolution" of this or that aspect of an organism—the brain, say, or the gut, or the limbs, or whatever—without considering that none of these things could possibly have had an evolutionary history separate from that of the species in which they are embedded. In sum, it is unrealistic to look on evolution as a matter of fine-tuning organisms or their components over vast periods of time. What we actually see in the fossil record is the (dimly reflected) histories of *species*.

What seems to happen, then, is that any successful and reasonably widespread species tends to diversify, developing local variants in different parts of its range. We routinely see this among species of the order Primates, the grand group of living things to which we belong together with the apes, monkeys, and lemurs. Primate species often include recognizably distinct subspecies in different geographical areas. The basis of this phenomenon is doubtless natural selection, at least in part; but it is probable that entirely haphazard influences are also important, for regional variants are likely to differ among themselves at least partly for reasons of random sampling. Subspecies are local populations that differ from other such populations in identifiable features and occupy their own geographic ranges. And, for a while at least, they will be definable in terms of their physical characteristics.

On the other hand, subspecies remain potentially ephemeral, for they will lose their identities if they are reabsorbed within the general population by interbreeding with other subspecies. Speciation—the establishment of a reproductive barrier between groups—is thus necessary if new variant populations are to become true historical entities. And speciation is not at all the same thing as the development of anatomical novelties of the kind that allow us to recognize different subspecies. Indeed, like evolution itself, speciation is not a single process. Essentially, it is a *result*—the inability or failure of individuals of two groups to reproduce; and this may come about in many ways, through differences at the level of the genes, or of the chromosomes into which genes are grouped, or even of anatomy or of behavior.

The fact that the creation of new species does not equate directly with anatomical change is unpopular with paleontologists, for it often makes it difficult to identify species in the fossil record with any confidence. This is because morphology—an organism's physical form—is essentially the only thing that paleontologists have to go by in making such judgments. The only other measurable attributes of fossils—their age and their geographic provenance—have an even more tenuous relationship to species identity than their physical form. In general, however, morphological differences between closely related species descended from the same parent species are not large, so the risk of not recognizing enough fossil species on the basis of anatomical differences will ordinarily be greater than that of recognizing too many.

In the end, though, despite the pivotal roles of speciation, competition, environmental change, and extinction in the evolutionary process, it remains true that evolution is also about the accumulation of inherited physical novelties over time in the packages we know as species. How does this happen? A new field, known by the nickname evo-devo (short for evolutionary developmental biology), is devoted to understanding how genetic innovations are related to patterns of physical change and has in recent years been making remarkable strides in this realm. While the evolutionary synthesis was being developed, the underlying assumption was that all genes acted in more or less the same ways, so the assumed gradual Darwinian evolution could be explained by averaging out the effects of several genes acting on each character. Now, however, developmental geneticists have discovered that not all genes are equal in determining physical outcomes. To be quite honest, it still is not entirely clear how genetic information is converted into living, adult beings; but it is known that although changes in most genes have small effects, those in some others may have dramatic effects on major developmental pathways.

Of particular interest here is a class of genes known as regulatory genes because they regulate development in the embryo by triggering (or suppressing) the activities of other sets of genes. The close similarity of many regulatory genes in organisms as disparate as insects, birds, and humans is a powerful argument for the evolutionary relatedness of these beings, as well as a reflection of the fundamental importance of such genes in the development of individual organisms. Genes of this kind are intricate in their workings, and their effects depend both on the interactions among genes and on the sequences in which they are switched on and off. Our increasing knowledge of regulatory genes has begun to shed light on how it is that organisms that appear to have radically different bodies can actually share common ancestry. What's more, it points to ways in which new forms of bodily organization can arise, not in a series of minute steps over vast spans of time but simply from changes in when and in what combination genes are switched on and off during the developmental process.

This is not only of interest to those who study the evolutionary relationships among the great contrasting groups of living things, but it also has implications for major organizational changes *within* smaller, closely related groups. A good example of the latter is the transition among hominids from the so-called archaic early upright-walking forms with small bodies, short legs, longish arms, and somewhat curved hands and feet, to tall, striding bipeds resembling our own species. This change was evidently an abrupt one. There are no known intermediate forms between the archaic and modern body structures, so it would seem that the latter appeared on the scene rather suddenly. We don't know exactly what genetic changes were involved in the shift from one body type to the other, but molecular and developmental geneticists are beginning to lift a corner of the curtain that lies over this mystery. And in the process they have provided a new set of reasons to revise our understandings of the evolutionary process as a slow, stately progression.

Every genetic novelty must, of course, arise in an individual. In his 1999 book *Sudden Origins*, University of Pittsburgh paleoanthropologist Jeffrey Schwartz broached the question of how such innovations can be transferred from the level of the individual in which they originate to that of the population to which that individual belongs. After all, if mutations do not make this move they will have no evolutionary future. Schwartz started from the observation that mutations that arise as dominant alleles tend to be bad for their possessors, and that successful—potentially advantageous—alleles hence tend to arise in the recessive state. Thus new recessive mutations could start to spread through the population—but invisibly, because they would not be expressed in the anatomies of heterozygous individuals (that is, those that possessed only one of the new alleles, along with a nonmutated allele).

In the early days of evolutionary theory, one idea proposed was that organisms of new kinds might arise as "hopeful monsters" resulting from a major mutation. This notion was roundly condemned on the grounds that such a "monster" would have no one to mate with. Under Schwartz's theory, however, finding a mate would not be a problem. And anyway, once a critical mass of externally normal heterozygotes was reached, recessive homozygotes—individuals with two copies of the recessive allele, who would thus exhibit the corresponding novel physical feature— would begin to turn up regularly in the population. And at this point natural selection could start to act, favoring one kind of physical form over the other.

Advances such as these are allowing us to glimpse how evolutionary theory—always a work in progress—is likely to develop over the next few decades. But what do they mean for our understanding of human evolution today? For a start, our growing understanding of how evolutionary processes function on a variety of levels is leading us to revise our expectations of what we will find as the expanding fossil record reveals the story of human evolution in ever greater detail. What are those expectations?

More than 2,000 years ago the Greek philosopher Aristotle saw human beings as occupying the highest rung of a great "ladder of being" that ultimately linked them with the most "lowly" life forms—pond scum and so forth—at the bottom. In medieval times, this idea was resuscitated by scholars who sandwiched humans in between God and the angels on top, and the other Earthly forms, from primates on down, below them. Oddly, this persistent notion suited many early evolutionists as well, at least those who saw gradualist Darwinian concepts as an explanation for the progression they perceived in the complexity of life. Paleoanthropologists inherited this notion as they assumed responsibility for interpreting the human fossil record and ultimately found that it was congenial to them, too.

We tend to take what is familiar for what is natural or for what should be, and there is only one hominid species on Earth today: *Homo sapiens*. Once the evolutionary synthesis had become widely accepted, then, it seemed reasonable to many to assume that the evolutionary story of mankind had consisted of a steady progression from primitiveness toward perfection. Indeed, during the 1960s there arose a school of thought that held that there could, in principle, only ever have been one hominid species on Earth at one time. Over the next couple of decades, however, it became clear from the growing fossil record that this was not the case: a few blind alleys, at least, had been explored by hominid

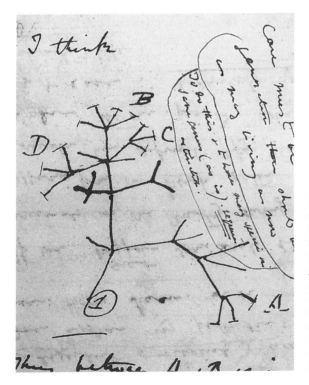

Darwin's sketch of an evolutionary tree of related creatures, from his private "Notebook B" of 1837. This is arguably the first diagram of its kind ever drawn, long before the publication of Origin of Species *in 1859. By permission of the Syndics of Cambridge University Library.*

species that had ultimately gone extinct. But nonetheless the linear idea persisted, and some still today defend the notion that there is a "main line" of human descent along which a gradual succession of species can be followed. According to this viewpoint, hominid fossils form links in a continuous chain (admittedly with the occasional side chain) that joins *Homo sapiens* with its remotest precursors.

With the arrival of the idea of punctuated equilibria and the understanding that species are fully individuated entities, playing evolutionary roles that go beyond simply being intermediates between their ancestors and descendants, some paleoanthropologists began to see the need to rethink this form of received wisdom. Discoveries made during the last quarter of the twentieth century and the beginning of the twenty-first have only served to accentuate this need. It is becoming increasingly apparent that the evolutionary history of the hominid family has not been a straightforward story of the fine-tuning of a major central lineage over the eons. Instead, it has been a dynamic saga in which multiple hominid species have originated, done battle in the ecological arena, and, more often than not, gone extinct. It has been a story of evolutionary experimentation, of exploration of the many ways in which it is evidently possible to be a hominid.

In earlier years, when the notion of the continuous chain held sway, it was possible to view fossils as a succession through time of links in that chain. Thus, if you knew the age of a hominid fossil you pretty much knew what place it occupied in human evolution. In this view paleoanthropology was essentially a business of discovery: find enough links and you would know how and where the chain ran. Now, however, we are beginning to realize that the business of the paleoanthropologist is a lot more complex than that. If species are unique entities defined by reproductive boundaries, we need first to recognize them in the fossil record. And our first order of business after that is to sort out their relationships. We cannot do this by discovery alone, much as we clearly need more fossils! Relationships have to be revealed by careful analysis, an enterprise that paleoanthropologists have only recently begun to undertake. Still, it is already abundantly clear that we have to view ourselves as one twig on a giant branching tree of life, rather than as below the angels on the highest rung of the ladder of being.

CHAPTER 2

Fossils and Ancient Artifacts

How do we know about our ancient ancestors, our forerunners from before the time when written records began to be kept (which, in evolutionary terms, is virtually yesterday)? For the very beginning of this story, all we have is the fossil record—the petrified remains of ancient animals and plants—and associated geological evidence about the times and environments in which those extinct precursors lived. For later stages we also have the archaeological record, the partial archive of the activities of our ancestors.

When an animal dies, its remains are usually scattered by wind, water, and scavengers and are then consumed or rot away. Occasionally, though, accumulating sediments—river or lake mud, for instance—may cover them and thus preserve them from immediate destruction. It is rare indeed for soft tissues such as muscles and organs to survive in the long term, but hard body parts (bones and teeth) that have been thus buried are sometimes preserved by fossilization. In this process, the organic components of the bones and teeth are replaced by minerals that, dissolved in water, filter through the enclosing sediments. In this way bones become literally turned to stone and will last indefinitely in the absence of external disruptions. The resulting fossils often contain an accurate record not only of the external form of the original bones and teeth, but also of their internal structures.

As a result of this history of preservation, fossils of ancient plants and animals can be found in sedimentary rocks, which are formed by particles that were eroded by wind and water from preexisting rocks and that become compressed and cemented together. Such sediments accumulate in successive layers. Fossils found low down in a sediment pile will thus be older than those found in layers above them. As a general rule, these layers form in a vertical sequence. But not infrequently entire sediment piles are tilted by earth movements and may even become folded back on themselves, so that the ideal "layer-cake" geological situation is rarer than one might wish. Rock sequences laid down in the seas tend to be fairly continuous over long periods of time. But those laid down on land are

The life history of a fossil. After death, most cadavers will be devoured by predators or scavengers (top left). What remains will either weather away or become buried in accumulating sediments (top right). In the right conditions such remains will become fossilized as their constituents are replaced by minerals acquired from the surrounding rock (bottom left). If erosion then wears away the overlying sediments, the fossil will be reexposed at the surface (bottom right), where someone must find it before it is destroyed by the elements. Artwork by Diana Salles, from Ian Tattersall, *The Human Odyssey* (1993).

typically incomplete, as lakes dry up and rivers change their courses, and as land is uplifted or sinks, changing zones of sediment deposition into areas of erosion and vice versa. All of these factors, and many more, conspire to complicate the work of geologists and paleontologists.

But the sedimentary record is more than just a fossil repository, for in any given place it also carries the signs of regional climatic and topographic history, as well as those of the changing panorama of local life. The characteristics of particular sedimentary rocks, for example, can tell geologists whether they were laid down by fast-moving or stagnant water, or by wind in a relatively vegetation-free environment. And the nature of the fossils found in a particular sedimentary environment can yield much information about what life was like in a region at any particular point in time.

How do we know exactly when the events reflected in the geological record occurred? For more than a century after the field of geology got started, it was impossible to assign ages in years to particular sedimentary layers and their contained fossils. All that geologists could do was to say that, in any given sedimentary basin, the deeper layers were older than those higher up. But such sedimentary sequences can be isolated and discontinuous; how can we correlate them? The traditional solution was to compare the fossils they contained. Early geologists quickly realized that different periods of the Earth's history were characterized by different fossil plants and animals. Rocks in different places but containing the same types of plants and animals were likely to be of similar age, whereas rocks with radically different floras and faunas probably represented different times. And although it is of course true that at any one time living things will differ from place to place (for instance, today we have polar bears in the Arctic and giraffes in the African tropics), geologists were rapidly able to piece together a broad picture of Earth's long history by correlating faunas from one region to another and by observing where they lie in relation to layers not containing fossils. This process is still ongoing, of course; but at this stage of the game geologists are mostly clearing up local details within an established worldwide timescale.

However, although the correlation of fossil plants and animals made it possible to decipher the sequence of events in the past—these fossils or rocks are older than those but younger than those others—it still did not permit geologists to assign ages in years to particular rocks and to the fossils they contained. And although procedures such as counting tiny annual layers of sediment that form in glacial lakes were tried early on, large-scale dating of ancient rocks and fossils had to await the mid-twentieth-century invention of radiometric dating. This approach makes use of the fact that certain radioactive isotopes (roughly, variant forms of particular elements), which are contained either within dead organisms themselves or within volcanic rocks that are in sequence with them, decay at known and constant rates. Such isotopes have unstable nuclei that spontaneously change (decay) to stable (unchanging) forms, at characteristic and constant rates. If you know what an isotope's decay rate is, it is possible to use it to calculate the amount of time that has elapsed since an organism died or since a volcanic rock cooled.

The best known way of dating fossils themselves is the radiocarbon method. All living organisms contain a certain amount of carbon, of which a known proportion is radioactive. As long as an organism is alive, the ratio of stable to radioactive carbon remains constant; but once the organism dies, the radioactive portion is no longer renewed and its amount begins to diminish relative to its stable cousin. The proportions of the two kinds of carbon in a sample will thus indicate how much time has elapsed since the organism died.

The half-life of radioactive carbon (the time it takes for half of the existing atoms to decay) is rather short, at less than 6,000 years, so by the time 40,000 to 50,000 years have elapsed there will be too little of it left to measure. This places a rather low maximum age on the fossils that can be dated using this technique; but radiocarbon, the first method of radiometric dating to be introduced, is still actively used in dating relatively recent fossils, such as those of *Homo neanderthalensis* and early *Homo sapiens*. It has, indeed, become particularly useful since the introduction of a variant method (accelerator mass spectrometry, or AMS dating) that allows tiny samples of organic material to be dated. As long as the samples being analyzed are of high purity, radiocarbon dating produces quite accurate results, although the measurements do need to be calibrated to compensate for factors such as varying radioactive carbon production in the upper atmosphere and shifts in the strength of Earth's magnetic field.

Other approaches to dating fossils directly include one known as electron spin resonance (ESR), for which tooth enamel is a favorite material (bone is not a good subject). Empty "traps" in the crystal structure of the enamel fill up with free electrons at a rate that varies with the background radiation level of the particular site where the fossil has rested. If that rate is known, then the number of electron traps that have been filled can be measured and used to calculate the time—up to 2 million years—since the traps were last empty, usually at the point when the organism died. This method can also be applied to the time of deposition of flowstones, which are layers of calcite that are often found in caves formed in limestone landscapes.

Another kind of trapped-charge dating is thermoluminescence (TL), which measures the light emitted by escaping electrons as a sample is heated. The amount of light is proportional to the number of emptying electron traps, which, again, have filled at a rate determined by background radiation. Because the traps empty when a sample is heated, this method can be applied to materials such as quartz and flint that for one reason or another were burned in campfires made by our precursors. Fortunately, the TL method works for the entire period during which ancient humans have been regularly using fire, and it has also been used to date the quartz in sands whose electron traps had been emptied by exposure to sunlight.

Perhaps the most widely used method of radiometric dating, particularly in older periods and where volcanism was rife, dates not the fossils themselves but, rather, the rocks within which they are found. This is the potassium/argon (K/Ar) technique, which in the early 1960s was the first technique to reveal the extraordinarily great age of ancient hominid fossils found in East Africa. Volcanic rocks contain potassium, a tiny but constant fraction of which is radioactive and decays very slowly to a stable form of the rare gas argon; the radioactive potassium has a half-life of 1.3 billion years. Volcanic rocks can contain no argon at the high temperatures at which they reach the Earth's surface, so any argon we measure in those rocks must have accumulated after the time at which the volcanic layers were laid down at or close to the surface and then cooled and began trapping argon. Thus, if we can measure the abundance of argon and potassium in our sample, we can calculate how long it has been since the rock cooled down. And although fossils do not generally occur directly in volcanic rocks, they may be common in the other rocks that are their neighbors in a sediment pile. So in a continuous sequence of sedimentary-rock layers we can guess quite reliably that fossils found just above or below a volcanic layer are a little bit younger or older than the datable rock. In recent years, the original K/Ar technique has been supplanted by a related method known as argon/argon (Ar/Ar), using argon gas extracted from individual mineral crystals and avoiding many of the technical pitfalls associated with earlier approaches.

Most of the human evolutionary story took place within the geological epochs known as the Pliocene (5.2 through 1.8 million years ago) and Pleistocene (1.8 million through 10,000 years ago). And it has long been known that the Pleistocene epoch, in particular, was marked in northern latitudes by successive episodes of climatic cooling and glaciation, in which the polar ice cap expanded vastly in the area it covered. In Europe such expansion covered northern Germany and most of England with ice hundreds of feet thick; in North America, during the last such glacial episode the ice sheet advanced as far south as what is now New York City.

Late in the nineteenth century it was proposed that the major European glacial episodes fell into a sequence of four cold spells, separated by warmer interglacial periods. This provided a convenient chronological framework into which fossils could potentially be fitted, but numerous problems emerged. The worst difficulty was posed by the fact that advancing ice sheets scour away the landscape over which they move; and then, when they melt, the debris gathered up by the ice is washed away and dumped elsewhere. In other words, ice sheets tend to destroy much of the evidence for their own passage, and it is very difficult to correlate evidence for glaciation in one place with that in another.

Fortunately, since the 1950s an efficient way of tackling the Pleistocene sequence of warmings and coolings has emerged. This capitalizes on the fact that, unlike land surfaces, seabeds contain a more or less unbroken record of sediment accumulation over time. And these sediments also contain the remains of forams, microorganisms whose "tests" (hard outer coverings) provide a record of the temperature of the sea at the time they lived. In their lifetimes, forams absorb two different isotopes of oxygen from the surrounding water. In cold times the seawater is richer in the heavier isotope, whereas when it gets warmer the lighter isotope increases. So when scientists drill vertical rock cores from the seafloor, they are recovering a continuous record of climatic change that can be read by isotopic analysis of the foram shells in the cores. This record can then be calibrated for time by combining several different methods of dating. Among these is paleomagnetism, a technique that exploits the fact that Earth's magnetic field periodically changes its direction.

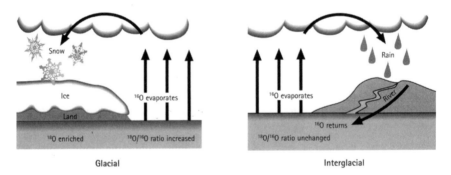

Glacial   Interglacial

Oxygen-isotope analysis. Past climates are reflected in the ratio of the oxygen isotopes ^{16}O and ^{18}O that are incorporated in the tests ("shells") of dead microorganisms that are found in sediment cores taken from the seafloor. These isotopes were acquired during life from the seawater in which the organisms floated. Since the lighter ^{16}O evaporates more readily from seawater and is returned to the sea in reduced quantities when precipitation becomes "locked up" in icecaps, in colder times this isotope becomes rarer in the seas when compared to ^{18}O. Artwork by Diana Salles, after Tjeerd Van Andel, New Views on an Old Planet *(1994), with permission.*

Today, our compass needles point north. But a million years ago they would have pointed south; and rocks, including the seabed cores, preserve a record of the direction of the magnetic field at the time they were laid down. Since the Pleistocene began there have only been four magnetic reversals, but the record in seabed cores shows that climate has fluctuated much more frequently. Thus, a complete calibration of the climatic record from the cores requires additional dating methods. One of these extrapolates lapses of time from sediment thicknesses; another invokes various aspects of Earth's elliptical orbit around the sun and the tilt of the axis on which it spins—factors that affect the amount and distribution of energy received from the sun, which in turn have important effects on climate.

The upshot of all this is that we now know that a gradual and unsteady climatic cooling during the past several million years climaxed in the Pleistocene, when the world was colder than at any point since about 200 million years ago. The Pleistocene was particularly remarkable for its climatic instability. By the time the Pleistocene began, about 1.8 million years ago, world climates had already become colder and more seasonal, the poles cooling off and winters in higher latitudes becoming longer and harsher. By about 500,000 years ago, the world had settled into a cyclical pattern of change in which climates cycled from warmer (such as at present) to much colder, with maximum expansions of the polar ice sheets about every 100,000 years or so. Although on average Pleistocene climates were significantly colder than those of today, each of these major shifts was marked by numerous smaller-scale climatic oscillations.

Thus today, instead of talking in sweeping terms about major glacial periods, scientists have developed a timescale for the later Pleistocene that involves a sequence of "isotopic stages," many of them quite short, and some of which are themselves subdivided into substages. Thus the relatively warm period between about 130,000 and 115,000 years ago is known as stage 5e, and was followed by cooler stages 5d through 5a, between 115,000 and 75,000 years ago. As the world continued to cool, stages 4 and 3 occurred between 75,000 and 30,000 years ago, and a period of lowest average temperatures (the "glacial maximum" of this cycle) constitutes stage 2, between about 30,000 and 12,000 years ago. In Europe the predominant vegetation during phases such as stage 5e would in many places have been oak and beech forests, much as at present, whereas in stages 3 through 4 the landscape would have been open, with vast numbers of herding animals grazing on grasses and low bushes. As we go farther back in time the climatic record becomes a little

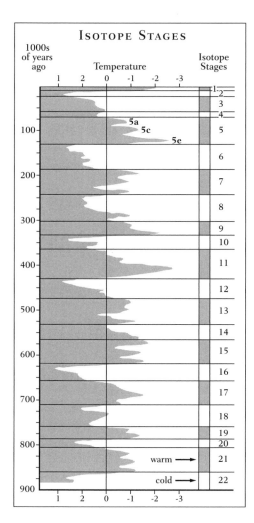

ISOTOPE STAGES

The oxygen isotope record of changing temperatures for the past 900,000 years, based on drilled cores taken from the Indian and Pacific Ocean seabeds. Temperatures are derived from the $^{16}O/^{18}O$ ratios in the cores, shown on the left of the diagram. Even-numbered isotope stages were relatively cool periods, whereas the odd-numbered ones were relatively warm. There were considerable temperature oscillations within each major stage. Based on the results of ODP deep-sea core 677 (from Shackleton and Hall, 1989, in K. Becker et al., *Proceedings of the ODP, Scientific Results*, vol. 111)

fuzzier, but the same trend is apparent. In stage 6, between about 180,000 and 130,000 years ago, the European subcontinent was for much of the time in the grip of full glacial conditions, but in the preceding stage 7 the climate was kinder, with cool temperate conditions reigning for much of the time.

The climatic irregularity of the ice ages affected not only the habitats in which our precursors lived, but the geography of their world as well. For as the ice sheets expanded, they "locked up" water that would previously have run off into the oceans, lowering sea levels and thus uniting many landmasses that are now separated by water barriers. As the ice caps contracted the reverse occurred, yielding shorelines more like those with which we are (temporarily) familiar today. Such geographically, climatically, and ecologically unstable conditions are, of course, precisely those most propitious for evolutionary innovation and change.

The fossils found at any given place can tell us quite a lot about the history of life in that particular locality. And fossils not only help to tell us how old specific rocks happen to be, but they can carry valuable information about former environments. For many species tend to have quite strong environmental preferences and thus to be quite sensitive indicators of the kind of habitat in which they formerly lived. But it is important to bear in mind that most fossil faunas are "death assemblages" rather than "life assemblages." In other words, the fossils you find in a particular place are not necessarily a representative sample of the animals that lived in the immediate environment. Sometimes, indeed, fossil bones show signs of having been transported by water far from the place where their possessors had died, so that the fossils found together are not necessarily those of animals that had lived together. Indeed, fossil bone assemblages within the same sedimentary basin may well sample several different environments or at least microenvironments.

What is more, factors other than water transport may also be involved in the sorting process. For example hyenas, which transport carcasses to their dens, have been a notable influence upon what fossils we find. Many hominid fossils have been found in what have turned out to be ancient hyena dens—which often resulted in rather fanciful interpretations of the resulting bone accumulations before their true nature was recognized. For example, a skull of *Homo neanderthalensis* that was found in an ancient hyena den at the Guattari Cave in Italy in 1939 was initially thought to have been severed from its body and deliberately placed in the center of a ring of stones and animal bones in some bizarre hominid ritual. Leopards, which tend to hoard their prey in particular trees, have apparently played a similarly significant role in the accumulation of hominid fossils, especially in earlier times in Africa.

It is also important to bear in mind that the fossil record as we know it is a rather biased representation of life in past eras. What we have found of the record of ancient life has largely been conditioned by geological accident. It's not easy to become a fossil in the first place; once fossilized, it takes enormous luck to make it onto a paleontologist's workbench. Rocks that contain hominid fossils are very spottily exposed at the Earth's surface, so what we have is a very selective sampling of our precursors. This makes the process of reconstructing our biological history rather like doing a jigsaw puzzle with only a fraction of the pieces—and no picture on the box! Indeed, it has been estimated that perhaps only some 3 percent of all of the primate species that have ever existed are represented by known fossils.

All of this makes it particularly important that we analyze the fossils at hand in appropriate ways. If, for example, we erroneously assume that evolution is essentially a process of fine-tuning in lineages of organisms that run like a chain through time, we are likely to want to cram all of the hominid fossils we find into that chain, as successive links. Taking this to its extreme, once you have determined which purported chain a fossil belongs to, its evolutionary place is determined essentially by its age, in a kind of connect-the-dots exercise. And if most of the links in the chain are missing anyway, the underlying deficiencies in this kind of scheme may not be readily apparent. This was for years the case in paleoanthropology, and the field is still recovering from its effects.

Sorting fossils into species isn't easy, and neither is the next step in the analysis—namely, determining which species are most closely related to each other. Each organism possesses a large number of different characteristics, but not all of these are equally useful in determining relationships. "Primitive" features, inherited from a remote common ancestor, may greatly affect the overall resemblance we see between two creatures, but they are not of much use in determining relationships within large groups whose members all share this ancestor. For the latter, you have to turn to what are called derived characters, which are inherited from more recent common ancestral forms. The sharing of unique derived characters is the central clue to which pairs of forms are most closely related to each other. So far, so good, even though all this can be complicated by the independent acquisition of similar characteristics, which may not be uncommon among closely related and therefore genetically similar forms.

But a real problem arises when you try to determine exactly what sort of relationship is involved. This is because relationships can be of two kinds: that between an ancestral species and its descendant and that between two species both descended from the same ancestor. These different categories of relationship have decidedly different implications for evolutionary histories, but it is difficult to distinguish between them even theoretically, especially where ancestry and descent are involved. This is because any ancestor obviously has to be primitive in all of its characteristics relative to its putative descendant; but when a form is primitive in everything, there will be no derived characteristics available to link it to its presumed relative!

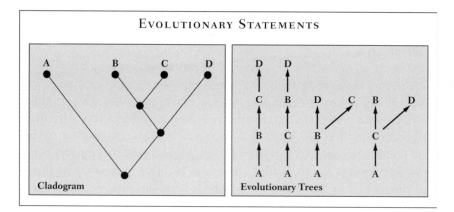

EVOLUTIONARY STATEMENTS

Cladogram

Evolutionary Trees

Statements of evolutionary relationship may be of two kinds. On the left is a cladogram, *a branching diagram that shows how closely different living forms are related by common ancestry. On the right is a set of* evolutionary trees, *which are statements of ancestry and descent among those forms. Because ancestry is a less testable proposition than simple relationship by descent from a common ancestor is, there is more room for argument among trees. All of the trees on the right are compatible with the cladogram on the left.* From Ian Tattersall and Niles Eldredge (1977).

All this might seem a little bit like worrying about how many angels can dance on the head of a pin, but it actually has a very important consequence for those who try to reconstruct evolutionary histories. For although a hypothesis of general relationship—that two species are more closely related to each other than either is to any other member of the larger group—can be tested on the basis of shared derived characters, questions of ancestry and descent cannot be. So in moving from the straightforward branching diagram known as a cladogram that shows generalized relationships, to the more complex formulation known as a phylogenetic tree that indicates specific ancestry and descent, you are moving away from the realm of testable science and into that of speculation, albeit informed.

When you go even further afield, to generate what is called a scenario by adding to the tree everything you know or think you know about environment, adaptation, and so forth, you are getting even farther away from testable science. Of course, fully fleshed-out scenarios are the most interesting kind of evolutionary story, and paleoanthropology would be rather tedious without them. But they need to be based on specified cladograms and trees if other scientists are to see where you are coming from; and the problem has been that paleoanthropologists have tended to dive in at the deep end, going directly to full-fledged scenarios. This has tended to reduce discussion in the field to a sort of storytelling competition.

The inherent interest of scenarios, of course, is that they bring fossils back to life, reinvesting the static bones with the features that once animated them. And if paleontology is not about past life, it's not about anything. Not only do fossil assemblages, properly interpreted, yield valuable information about time, environments, and the competing species with which each denizen had to cope, but, viewed with an engineer's eye, individual fossils can tell us a lot about how the individuals they represent had functioned in life. Limb proportions, joint surfaces, muscle attachments, dental characteristics, and a host of other features can reveal a great deal about physical behaviors. It bears repeating here, however, that it is wise to steer well clear of the notion that all or most species are incredibly fine-tuned to their environments—after all, specialist species tend to have much higher extinction rates than generalists do.

For times before we have an archaeological record, any evidence bearing on the lifestyles of our precursors is entirely inferential. Ways of life have to be reconstructed almost entirely from analyses of how a particular bodily structure would have worked, using analogies of living organisms with similar structures. Indeed, apart from a few studies that have revealed a rather carnivore-like chemical "signature" in the bones of some of our very remote predecessors, there is nothing direct at all to go on in determining the behaviors of the most ancient hominids. But with the appearance of the archaeological record everything changes, and we begin to have a source of information about what our ancestors actually did during their lives that is independent of inference from bodily form.

The archaeological record begins with the first stone tools that early hominids left behind them, at places where those tools were used to cut up the carcasses of dead animals. In this connection, it may be useful to note that hominids may not be the only kinds of animal with an archaeological record: in West Africa, researchers have discovered that over several generations ancient chimpanzees evidently used stones as anvils for nut cracking. For in the strictest sense, an archaeological record accumulates wherever there is tangible evidence left behind of any kind of behavior; and it just happens that such records are almost always formed only where the behaviors concerned involve the manipulation of hard materials that preserve in the geological record.

Effectively, however, archaeological sites are an exclusively hominid phenomenon; even from the earliest periods they consist not just of the stone tools themselves but of the bones of animals the tools were used to cut and of the way in which artifacts and bones were scattered around. When intensive study of the earliest archaeological sites began in the late 1960s, there was a tendency to interpret them as the leavings of creatures who were essentially junior-league versions of ourselves. Sites with stone tools and broken bones were regarded as home bases, to which hominids returned. In one case a 2-million-year-old circle of rocks that had been shattered and scattered in a circle by the roots of a growing tree was interpreted as a windbreak or a rudimentary form of shelter.

Archaeologists soon realized that this kind of reading was a little fanciful, investing very early hominids with more extensively "human" attributes than was perhaps wise; but especially as our studies move up in time, to hominids who were undoubtedly increasingly similar to us, we still need to resist the temptation to interpret them in our own image. No matter how much we may have had in common with the Neanderthals, it is still a profound mistake to assume that their way of perceiving and interacting with the world resembled our own.

For the Paleolithic, or Old Stone Age (a period stretching between about 2.5 million and 10,000 years ago, before humans began building in stone), archaeological sites consist of little more than what hominids threw away or just left behind them. Not for nothing has Paleolithic archaeology been called "the study of ancient garbage." The very earliest archaeological sites are not stratified into layers; they were simply spots on the landscape at which hominids had paused, used tools, and moved on. As time passed, archaeological sites increasingly become favored places where hominids returned repeatedly, even if at long intervals. In such cases a succession of layers would accumulate, characterized by strata containing the remnants of hominid activities, interspersed with plain beds of naturally accumulating sediment. In some cases, sediment piles of this kind grew up to many meters thick, eventually entirely filling up cave entrances or shelters where overhangs of rock afforded some natural protection from the elements. The myth of the "cave man" derives from the fact that such places were both favored spots for hominids to camp and locations where their debris was likely to be preserved. In fact, ancient *Homo* rarely if ever lived deep in caves, and if they ever did shelter there, they nonetheless spent most of their lives out in the open.

As time passed, the contents of hominid living sites became more elaborate. But because only hard materials are preserved over time, what has come down to archaeologists is but a pale and distant reflection of the full behavioral ranges of the hominids who left the items behind.

Much of hominid material culture (objects made by people) has doubtless always consisted of artifacts made from soft materials that begin to rot away almost immediately; and material culture itself reflects only a fraction of the many behaviors of any group. Indeed, before the advent of writing, most hominid behaviors left no record at all. It is all the more important, then, to avoid filling in the gaps by assuming that earlier hominids communicated, thought, or viewed the world in ways that closely resembled our own. Close relatives though many were, they were different species, and we can be sure that none of them interacted with the external world exactly or even approximately as we do.

So when we use the words "human" and "hominid," what exactly do we mean? This is a perennial difficulty that is not going to go away anytime soon. People have been referring to themselves as "human" since long before they realized that we are related to the living apes, let alone that we have many closer relatives that are now extinct. Until quite recently, then, the perceived gap between human beings and the rest of nature was so wide that the word "human" hardly needed definition: its meaning was self-evident. But with the realization that this gap is indeed in some sense bridged by other species, the question of where we draw the limits of "humanity" has taken on real significance. Exactly how much significance is debatable, though, and it is likely that paleoanthropologists will remain splendidly inconsistent in their use of the term. "Human evolution," for instance, is generally taken to refer to the evolution of all those forms that are more closely related by common ancestry to our own species, *Homo sapiens,* than they are to any of the living apes. In this sense, human evolution is the study of the origins and evolution of the zoological family Hominidae, the formal category to which we and they belong.

But even here we have to be careful. Zoologists classify living forms into a hierarchy with many different levels. The basic unit is the species, such as *Homo sapiens*. The two-part species name starts with the name of the genus (in our case, *Homo*), the larger category into which closely related species are grouped. All species in the same genus bear the same genus name, whereas the second name can occur in any number of genera; thus it is the combination of names that is unique. Genus and species names are always written in italics, except by the *New York Times*, but the names of larger groupings are always given in regular (roman) type. Genera are grouped into subfamilies, which in turn are grouped into families, superfamilies, orders, and so forth, as we move up the hierarchy. Unlike military-style hierarchies, in which an individual can only have a single rank (private, lieutenant, colonel, and so on), the hierarchy of zoological classification is inclusive, meaning that each rank also includes all those below it. Thus the species *Homo sapiens* belongs to the subfamily Homininae of the family Hominidae of the order Primates, and so on.

The system of classification of living things that we use today was invented by the Swedish biologist Carolus Linnaeus in the mid-eighteenth century and was based on the pattern of similarities that Linnaeus and his colleagues observed among the denizens of the living world. Although in the earliest days zoological names were often descriptive, their current purpose is strictly one of identification. To avoid confusion, the choice of names is governed by elaborate rules. In its original, pre-Darwinian form the Linnaean hierarchy had relatively few ranks, but the number of these has multiplied as our knowledge of organisms living and extinct has grown. The "family" developed subfamilies and superfamilies, for instance, while at a lower level, tribes and even subtribes and supertribes have intervened between the genus and family levels. Groups at any level of the hierarchy can be referred to as "taxa" (singular: taxon).

At least in part, the multiplication of ranks in the taxonomic hierarchy has been necessitated by the desire to keep taxa monophyletic, which means that each taxon should consist only of the descendants of the same common ancestor. However, even with a large number of ranks available it is not always possible to reflect all of the (changeable) minutiae of descent in a classification, and many consider it unwise to try to do so. Classifications are essentially reference devices that are most useful when they remain stable, and this purpose is usually best served by insisting that although taxa should be monophyletic, they need not necessarily include *all* of the descendants of the common ancestral form. Some conventions have been developed to make it easier to navigate the mass of names in the Linnaean system. For example, subfamily names always end in "-inae," family names in "-idae," and superfamily names in "-oidea."

With the arrival of evolutionary theory in the mid-nineteenth century, it was realized that the groups-within-groups structure evident in the living world (we know intuitively that we are more closely related to a monkey than to a cow, and that all three of us are more closely related to each other than any of us is to a shark) is the result of a pattern of steadily diversifying ancestry and descent. Happily, this pattern is quite appropriately represented by the system of hierarchical classification, which was invented in the eighteenth century, 100 years before Darwin. Thus all primates are descended from a fairly ancient single ancestor, as, more recently, is each of the various families within our order and each of the genera within each family.

There is some debate over whether it is actually appropriate to classify *Homo sapiens* and its extinct relatives together in the family Hominidae to the exclusion of all of the living great apes (gorillas, bonobos, chimpanzees, and orangutans). For it turns out that we and our fossil relatives might be more closely related to one of these great apes than to the others (chimpanzees and bonobos are the current frontrunners, but there are other active contenders). There is consequently argument over whether Hominidae should contain some or all of the great apes as well as humans and their relatives, and there are those who would reduce Hominidae as accepted here to the subfamily Homininae or even to the tribe Hominini. The details of this debate are as obscure as they are numerous, but perhaps it is enough to point out that there is by now enough genus- and species-level diversity documented within the taxon, or classification group, containing *Homo sapiens* and its non-ape close relatives to justify regarding it as a full-

An outline classification of our species. The rules of zoological classification produce an inclusive, rather than an exclusive, hierarchy, so that a taxon (group) belongs to all of the larger categories that lie above it. Thus *Homo sapiens* belongs to both the infraorder Catarrhini and to the order Primates.

Order	**Primates** lemurs and lorises, tarsiers, monkeys, apes, humans
Suborder	Haplorhini tarsiers, monkeys, apes, humans
Hyperorder	Anthropoidea Old and New World monkeys, apes, humans
Infraorder	Catarrhini Old World monkeys, apes, humans
Superfamily	Hominoidea great and lesser apes, humans
Family	Hominidae humans and their extinct relatives
Genus	*Homo*
Species	*Homo sapiens*

fledged zoological family in itself. Thus, for our purposes "human evolution" is synonymous with the evolutionary history of the family Hominidae.

Still, this does not solve the problem of what "human" means in a functional sense. The earliest hominids, for example, were certainly not beings whom we would instinctively recognize as "human." And even the earliest members of the genus *Homo* might not qualify for this description were we to meet one of them in the flesh. Indeed, there is a strong argument to be made that among our departed relatives only those very recent ones who behaved more or less exactly in the ways we do today could be regarded as "fully human." The important thing to remember is thus that there are no absolute rights or wrongs in the debate over the definition of "human" and that each one of us may quite legitimately have a different perspective on the matter.

On Their Own Two Feet

Not everyone agrees about when, exactly, the family Hominidae came into existence—that is, when the last ancestor of *Homo sapiens* lived that was not also the ancestor of one or more of the great apes. Partly this is because the ancient fossil record of the hominids is sparse; partly it is because what there is of that record is difficult to interpret; and partly it is because there is no precise agreement right now on how much time the molecular (DNA) differences that have so far been measured among the living hominoids (humans and the greater and lesser apes) tell us has elapsed since our lineage went its own way. Still, we have made progress. In 1950, nobody had the slightest idea in calendar terms about how far back into time the hominid family could trace its roots. The techniques necessary for making an estimate in years simply weren't there. But in the 1960s, after the arrival of chronometric dating methods, it came to be widely believed that some fragmentary fossils from India and Kenya, 12 to 14 million years old and known variously as *Ramapithecus* and *Kenyapithecus*, might be the remains of a human precursor.

Even as this notion was weakening under the onslaught of new fossil discoveries, scientists in the emerging field of molecular systematics (in which molecular structures rather than anatomical ones are compared in order to determine zoological affinities) made an astonishing counterclaim, arguing for a much more recent point of hominid emergence, perhaps as little as 5 million years ago. In the last quarter of the twentieth century there was some convergence of such estimates, mostly toward the shorter end of the scale, with the paleontologists abandoning the notion of extreme hominid antiquity, and the molecular systematists easing up in their insistence on its great youth. Most observers, whatever kind of data they are dealing with, are relatively content at present with the notion that the last common ancestor of human beings and of one or more of the apes lived around 7 million years ago, give or take a million years or so. But this is a fluid number and not one that is likely to solidify any time soon.

Not very long ago there were no fossil contenders for hominid status that dated to more than 3 to 4 million years ago. Now, thanks to active fieldwork and some remarkable discoveries, there are several candidates in the 4- to-7-million-year range. Still, the picture remains a little murky, not least because we are not entirely sure what to expect that our earliest ancestor looked like. In considering this matter, paleoanthropologists have traditionally started by contemplating themselves. We human beings differ from our closest living relatives in a variety of respects, and during the last century or so several different human peculiarities have been taken as *the* defining characteristic of humanity.

Among the most obvious distinctive human characteristics is our large brain, three times the volume (even relative to body size) of that of any ape. Early paleoanthropologists were particularly entranced by this symbol of human superiority, so much so that almost all of them were prepared to be taken in by the Piltdown hoax, sprung in 1911. The supposedly very ancient skull found at Piltdown, in southeastern England, was eventually exposed as a fabrication that combined a recent human braincase with a modern ape jaw. But for the almost half-century before the fraud was exposed, this "specimen" stood as powerful testimony that an enlarged brain had been the key human feature from the very beginning—even once evidence began to accumulate that it had not been.

Once the enlarged human brain had lost its glamour in this regard, scientists began to look elsewhere for the human hallmark. Our precision grip (key to the venerable notion of "man the toolmaker") and our very small canine teeth (great apes' canines are rather large, especially in males) were both considered and ultimately rejected as uniquely diagnostic criteria. Researchers eventually focused their attention on our upright, two-legged posture, which is nowadays almost universally considered to be the defining characteristic of the human lineage. Nothing that was not an upright biped could be considered hominid. Of course there was a logical flaw here, for our expectation is no more than an assumption. What we need to do is to demonstrate that a fossil candidate for hominid ancestry is not excluded from that position by any of its characteristics, not to demonstrate that it has passed some predefined threshold that is based on a derived characteristic of later hominids. Navel-gazing aside, though, the search for the first hominid has in practice boiled down over the past few decades to the search for the first upright biped. And the problem has become that few if any of the fossils recently claimed to be very early hominids have (at this writing) a clearly demonstrable bipedal form.

This cranium of Sahelanthropus tchadensis, *a putative early hominid from Chad, in central-western Africa, is between 6 and 7 million years old; it is currently the most ancient claimant to membership in the hominid family.* Courtesy of Michel Brunet.

The very earliest fossil to have been described as a hominid is a cranium (skull minus the lower jaw) that was found in Chad, in central-western Africa, a discovery announced in 2002. It is believed to be about 6 to 7 million years old. Not only is this an extraordinarily early date for a hominid, but the specimen comes from a decidedly unexpected place: almost all other early African hominids have been discovered thousands of miles to the east, in the Rift Valley region of eastern Africa, and in South Africa.

Sahelanthropus tchadensis, as the skull has been named in reference to where it was found, is surprising in its morphology, too. To give some context, when you compare the skull of, say, a chimpanzee to that of a human being, you first of all notice that the relationship between the facial skeleton and the braincase is totally different in the two species. In the chimp, the facial skeleton is large, projects forward prominently, and contains big jaws and teeth. It dwarfs the small braincase that sits behind it. In a gorilla, the braincase viewed from the side looks a bit bigger in proportion to the face than a chimpanzee's, but only because a large flange of bone (called the sagittal crest) projects vertically along the midline of the skull, making the braincase look bigger than it is. This ridge is there to compensate for a shortage on the small skull surface of muscle attachment area for the huge jaw muscles. In the human skull, in contrast, the small, flat face and jaws are tucked beneath the front of a huge, balloon-like braincase. The effect could not be more different.

In light of these comparisons, *Sahelanthropus* is odd. Its face is massive, but flat, with an oddly "modern" look to it, while its tiny braincase is very apelike, even bearing a trace of sagittal crest. It bears rather small canine teeth, and its describers have found evidence of a rather forward-placed foramen magnum. This last feature is the large hole in the base of the skull through which the spinal cord joins the brain; it is typically found beneath the skull in species with upright posture, whereas in four-legged animals it points more directly backward. Naturally, the discoverers of *Sahelanthropus* find hominid resemblances here, although these can be disputed. It is altogether an extraordinary specimen. So how does *Sahelanthropus* compare with other very early supposed hominids?

In the case of the other 6-million-year-old fossil candidate for classification as a hominid, it's a little hard to say. This is because the poorly known *Orrorin tugenensis*, discovered in 2000 in the Baringo Basin of northern Kenya, consists so far mostly of postcranial bones—that is to say, bits of the body skeleton. The bones in question are mostly parts of a couple of femora (thigh bones) and part of a humerus (upper-arm bone). And although there is nothing to dispute the assertion by the fossils' finders that the leg bones show features associated with upright walking, the parts really needed to confirm this have so far not been found. The few known teeth of *Orrorin*, described in 2001, are also not easy to interpret. The premolar and molar (chewing) teeth of other early hominids tend to be rather large, yet these are fairly small; so is the one known canine tooth, but in shape it is considered to be rather chimpanzee-like.

The picture is muddied yet further by another claimed early hominid also described in 2001. This is *Ardipithecus kadabba*, a name given to some fragmentary fossils from sites in Ethiopia dated to between 5.8 and about 5.2 million years ago. The *A. kadabba* scraps include a foot bone that is thought to indicate bipedality. But even if this is accurate, we should be wary of concluding that *Ardipithecus* was bipedal in any familiar way. The describer of a later (about 4.4 million years old) species of *Ardipithecus*, *A. ramidus*, warns that anyone wanting to find an analog for the way it walked should "check out the bar scene in *Star Wars*." The *A. ramidus* fossil material also includes teeth that are rather atypical for hominids. However, it has been said to represent an upright biped because it includes a fragment of cranial base that apparently shows a forward-positioned foramen magnum.

Where does all this leave us? We have a very motley assemblage of purported early hominid material from the period between 6-plus and 4.4 million years ago, and it may be significant that *Ardipithecus* has been compared with chimpanzees and *Sahelanthropus* with gorillas. But if all of these forms, or even some of them, are genuine hominids, they establish that from the very beginning the history of the human family has not been the single-minded slog from primitiveness to perfection so beloved of the devotees of the evolutionary synthesis. Rather, it has been a history of evolutionary experimentation, a process of exploration of the many different ways that there evidently are to be hominid. This is an important lesson for us to learn. The fact that *Homo sapiens* is the only hominid species on the Earth today makes it easy to assume that our lonely eminence is historically a natural state of affairs—which it clearly is not.

So what set this process of evolutionary experimentation in motion? Episodes of diversification within groups of organisms, often known as adaptive radiation, are frequently spurred by changes in the environment. And it appears that the hominid radiation was no exception. During most of the Miocene epoch, which ended about 5.2 million years ago, the African continent, in which the hominid family emerged, was largely covered by forests of various kinds. In these forests had flourished a diverse variety of hominoid primates, that is, members of the group from which both human and ape ancestors emerged. About 10.5 million years ago, polar cooling and a seasonal decline in rainfall toward the equator began to affect the African forest cover, leading to the gradual breakup of dense forests and the consequent spread of more open woodlands and grassy areas. Along with this change the diversity of the forest-living Miocene hominoids began to dwindle, and it is probably no coincidence that the hominid family began to establish itself just as more open habitats were becoming a significant part of the African landscape.

Clearly, though, hominids did not simply emerge out of the forests and onto the open savanna in one fell swoop (indeed, they could not have done so, for classic treeless Serengeti-type savannas were still very far in the future). Rather, they embarked on a long period of exploration of the possibilities offered by the new and expanding forest-edge and woodland habitats. The fossils of other mammals found along with those of the early hominids seem to confirm this preference for woodland environments, which have their own distinctive animal communities, although archaic hominid fossils have been found in contexts that indicate both relatively dense forest and quite open conditions. Possibly it was the exploration of varied habitats that was responsible for the apparent diversity of the earliest hominids.

The oldest hominid that we know for sure walked upright, at least when on the ground, is *Australopithecus anamensis*, a species known

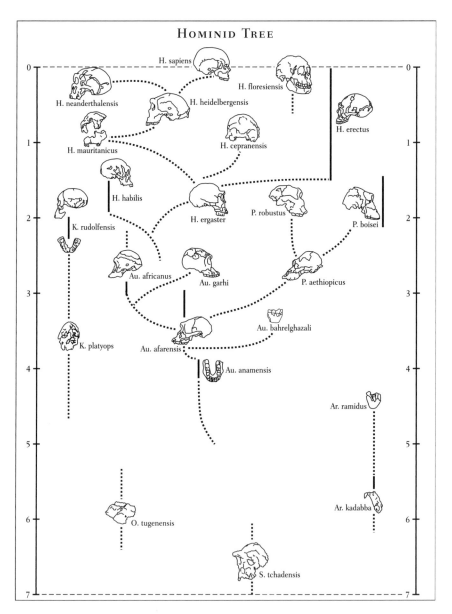

HOMINID TREE

A highly speculative phylogenetic tree of the family Hominidae, containing most of the fossil hominid species recognized by recent scholars. Dotted lines represent possible pathways of ancestry and descent, while solid lines connect the oldest and youngest current records of each species. Time runs along the vertical axis; horizontal arrangement is arbitrary. © Ian Tattersall.

from a small sample of fossils from the sites of Kanapoi and Allia Bay in northern Kenya. Nearly all of these fossils date from between 4.2 and 3.9 million years ago, and one of them consists of pieces of tibia (the lower-leg bone) that show clear signs of upright posture. When apes amble along on all fours, their legs go straight down to the ground from their hip joints, rather like table legs do. This is fine while the apes are supporting their weight on four limbs, but is a bit of a handicap when they try to walk on two legs because they have to swivel the outer leg around their center of gravity to take each step forward, swaying the body sideways in the process.

In contrast, an upright biped like ourselves has upper legs that slant inward toward the knee from the hip joints. In this way, with each stride the weight of the body is transmitted straight forward as the feet move close by each other, with no awkward sideways movement. Part of the apparatus needed to accomplish this lies in the knee joint, the surface of which is oriented at a right angle to the shaft of the tibia rather than with a sideways cant as in the apes. In the *A. anamensis* tibia, the part that contributes to the knee joint has the same orientation as in a human tibia, a pretty firm indication of upright posture. And there are equivalent indications in the ankle joint.

In those fossil bits that are known, *A. anamensis* is fairly comparable to *A. afarensis*, the best-known of all of the several early bipedal hominid species allocated to the genus. The most famous fossil representing the latter species, and probably the most famous hominid fossil of all time, is "Lucy," the partial, but nonetheless unusually complete, skeleton of a tiny (and thus presumed female) individual who lived 3.18 million years ago. Discovered in the mid-1970s at Hadar in Ethiopia, Lucy is one of many fossils thought to belong to this species that have been found at sites as far from Ethiopia as Tanzania and possibly Chad, and that date from about 4 to 3 million years ago. Among these other fossils are two fairly complete skulls from 3-million-year-old deposits at Hadar, as well as postcranial bones that nicely complement what we know from Lucy herself. One remarkable find, from a 3.4-million-year-old stratum also at Hadar, is the "First Family," the fragmentary remains of as many as 13 individuals who may have died together in a natural catastrophe such as a flash flood.

From the resulting aggregate of fossils, we have a pretty good picture of what *A. afarensis* looked like and a lot of information on which to base guesses about the way in which these creatures moved around (which doesn't, of course, mean that all paleoanthropologists are in agreement on the matter!). The size range among the bones of mature

A. afarensis is particularly striking and implies that males were a great deal larger than females. Lucy herself probably stood little more than three feet tall, whereas males may have been a foot taller. Estimates of body weight vary; males may have weighed up to about 100 pounds, and females may not have exceeded 60 pounds.

The first thing you might notice about the skeleton of *A. afarensis* is its wide, shallow pelvis, which at first glance seems to be proportioned rather like our own. It certainly contrasts dramatically with the long, narrow pelvis of the quadrupedal apes. The pelvis of *A. afarensis* is not that of a quadruped that wore its innards slung as in a hammock beneath the spine. Instead, these organs were supported from below by the bony bowl of the pelvis (though not as effectively as in *Homo sapiens*). The broad, shallow pelvis therefore bespeaks an upright posture, though it doesn't tell us much about whether that posture was adopted mainly in the trees or on the ground.

In terms of moving around, the ape pelvis has a form that gives the thigh muscles their greatest mechanical advantage when the hip is flexed. In contrast, the human hip is arranged so that speed and the range of available movement are emphasized, particularly when the leg is extended straight out. The *A. afarensis* pelvis lies clearly on the human side of this divide, but it is not identical to our own. The ball-and-socket hip joint, for example, has a rather small surface area, which concentrates (rather than diffusing, as in humans) the force generated when the foot hits the surface being walked on. And the pelvis itself is remarkably wide and flaring, with numerous anatomical details that are not matched in any living form. Few would disagree that the *A. afarensis* pelvis shows a radical reorganization in the direction of uprightness when contrasted to the presumably more ancestral condition of apes, but its combination of features leaves much room for debate on exactly how the species moved around.

The hip joint of *A. afarensis* may leave questions unanswered, but the knee joint is more conclusive. The knee joint of Lucy and her kin was clearly that of an upright biped, whose thighs converged from the hips to the knee, just like ours and those of *A. anamensis*. This can be seen most dramatically in the distinct angle formed between the horizontal knee-joint surface and the inwardly angled axis of the femur shaft. The tibia went straight down from the knees to the feet, which would have passed close together when walking. Overall, though, the legs were shorter than ours relative to body size, and the bones of the feet in these archaic hominids do not tell a simple story. The rear of the foot is relatively short like ours, and it has features in common with later humans that indicate a restricted ability to move beyond the fore-and-aft plane. In front of the ankle, in contrast, the foot was longer than ours, especially in its frontmost part, where the bones of the toes can be described as particularly apelike.

How about the rest of the body? The arm bones of *A. afarensis* show both apelike and humanlike characteristics, and the arms themselves are longer than ours in comparison with the legs, though most of this disparity seems to be due to the shortness of the legs. The shoulders are narrow, and the rib cage is very unlike ours. Instead of being essentially cylindrical in shape when seen from the front, it tapers dramatically outward from top to bottom, as ape rib cages do. Viewed from the top, though, it is shallow from front to back as ours is, rather than being deep like that of a quadruped. The spine itself is composed of vertebrae with long projections for muscle attachment, indicating a relatively massive musculature. The muscles in this area of the body are important in locomotion among both quadrupeds and bipeds, though, so this doesn't help us much in determining posture. However, a telling indicator lies in the weight-bearing central parts of the back vertebrae. In *A. afarensis*, these are small relative to ours (and to those of apes); but in one related species, at least, the vertabrae show evidence that the spine (in side view) had

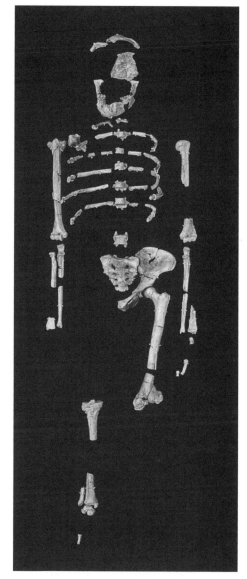

The skeleton of "Lucy" (from 3.18 million years ago), who was only about three feet tall. Courtesy American Museum of Natural History.

the double curve that is another characteristic of our upright posture.

So what do all these conflicting indicators add up to in telling us how *A. afarensis* got around? There has been a great deal of debate on this subject, with some paleoanthropologists emphasizing the evident specializations for bipedality that can be seen widely through the skeleton, and others placing more importance on the features retained from a tree-living past. However, some consensus seems to be emerging between the extremes. Researchers have reported that, particularly in relatively open environments, chimpanzees tend to hold their torsos upright while foraging in trees, and many think that hominids evolved from species that did the same thing with even greater frequency. On the ground the primarily quadrupedal chimpanzees fold their hands so as to bear the weight of their upper body on the outsides of their knuckles and have thereby been able to retain the long hands that are so useful to them in grasping tree branches. But, predisposed as they almost certainly were to holding their bodies upright anyway, the ancestral hominids took a different tack as the African forests began to fragment, walking upright on two legs as they moved across the ground.

This history resulted in animals that were not as agile in the trees as apes or as efficient on the ground as we are. Nonetheless, the have-your-cake-and-eat-it-too adaptation exemplified by A. afarensis evidently served this species and its relatives well, for it endured as a stable anatomical complex for several million years. Clearly, these early hominids were quite comfortable in the expanding forest fringe areas that offered the resources of both the deep forest and the more open woodlands. Occasionally they evidently ventured entirely into the open, as shown by the astonishingly preserved 3.5-million-year-old bipedal trackways of Laetoli, in Tanzania.

One intriguing suggestion is that, during these early times, hominids got their start as omnivores by using their arboreal skills to steal the antelope carcasses that leopards—denizens of the woodland and savanna—regularly stashed in trees precisely so that they would not be stolen while their owners were away roaming over the landscape. Chimpanzees are known to hunt monkeys and small antelopes, so there is no reason to suspect that the very earliest hominids would have been unfamiliar with the advantages of a high-protein diet.

Accordingly, right from the earliest days of their discovery, our ancient ancestors were interpreted as hunters, with an intrinsic propensity for violence. After all, human beings have historically been very successful hunters, and even chimpanzees hunt occasionally; so shouldn't the early "bipedal apes" have been hunters as well? Not necessarily. In the last half million years or so of human evolution, hunting has undoubtedly been critically important to the hominid way of life; but before that, the picture is much less easy to interpret. Early authors suggested that ancient hominid fossils and the animal bones found with them were the remains of the hunters and their victims, respectively. But in the 1980s, the paleontologist Bob Brain pointed out that the whole assemblage looked like the remains of leopard and hyena prey. Indeed, Brain found one australopith skull bearing puncture marks that were almost certainly made by the canine teeth of a leopard. And in their recent book *Man the Hunted*, the anthropologists Donna Hart and Bob Sussman have argued that being prey species shaped the early hominids far more than the occasional hunting of a hare would ever have done.

Hart and Sussman point out that early hominids, coming to the ground as their formerly forest habitat fragmented, were ecologically edge species, flourishing in those areas where the forest gave way to woodland and grassland. And today's most successful edge primates are not the apes but the macaque monkeys of Asia, adaptable generalists who live in large groups that usually split up into smaller subgroups for foraging. They are behaviorally flexible and omnivorous, and they tend to return to home bases each night. They are also subject to quite high levels of predation, which has a major influence on their group organization and movements.

While they are closer human relatives than macaques are, today's apes are very differently adapted from early hominids, and Hart and Sussman conclude that ecologically the macaque analogy may be a better one. So they propose that early hominids may have lived in multi-male, multi-female groups of variable size that split up during the day's activities, but re-formed at night at well-protected home bases, sleeping on cliffs and in the trees, a preference that fits well with their anatomies. The early hominids would have been omnivorous, eating fruit, herbs, roots, and the occasional insect or lizard. As in macaques, females formed the social core of the group, which was always vulnerable to predators. Males, who are reproductively more expendable, served as sentinels, and indeed it may have been the threat of predation in their new habitat that formed many of the behaviors of our small and relatively defenseless early ancestors. This is additional reason to believe that, while they may have preferred to move on their hind limbs over the ground, the early hominids had not emancipated themselves entirely from the trees. Indeed, it is very likely that at night these small-bodied and largely defenseless animals regularly took shelter in the relative safety of trees, cliffs, and other places accessible only to climbers.

The perennial question of "why bipedality?" has most frequently been posed in immediate functional terms, rather than in terms of the structure of the ancestral form from which the first hominid bipeds were descended. Paleoanthropologists have regularly tried to identify the "advantage" that assured the eventual triumph of bipedal hominoids in non-forest environments. It has been suggested, for example, that the key factor was the freeing of the hands that bipedalism allows. Once your hands are not committed to supporting your body weight, they are available to be modified and used for other purposes, such as carrying or manipulating objects. Similarly, it has been pointed out that by standing up you can see potential dangers at a greater distance. Or maybe bipedal locomotion was simply more efficient than quadrupedalism over open ground.

Some years ago the paleoanthropologist Owen Lovejoy caused quite a stir by suggesting that the success of the early bipeds was due to a reorganization of reproductive activity that increased the rate of production of offspring. Lovejoy pointed out that modern humans are unique among hominoids in two important ways. First, males have no way of knowing when females are ovulating (and thus ready to reproduce); and second, particular males and females tend to become long-term reproductive pairs. These traits, he thought, had roots deep in the hominid past. From the beginning, bipedalism freed the hands of females to carry extra babies around. However, the consequently limited mobility of the females required them to bond with males who would then use their freed hands to bring them food they had obtained. Of course, the only way for males to be certain that the infants they fed were their own was to develop pair bonds with certain females. And from the female point of view, constancy of male interest could be ensured only by the development of highly visible secondary sexual characteristics, such as prominent breasts, which serve as constant attractants, replacing the cyclical swelling around the genitalia that had previously served to attract males by advertising ovulation.

The key to the success of this strategy, Lovejoy believes, is that the energy saved by non-foraging females could be invested in extra reproductive effort. This hypothesis emphasizes bipedality as an adaptation for increasing reproductive fitness rather than as an efficient means of getting around or shedding heat, and it neatly links our peculiarities of locomotion, reproduction, and social organization. However, it has been convincingly contested on a whole host of grounds, among them that the great disparity in body size between males and females of *Australopithecus afarensis* is typical of polygynous hominoids (among whom males constantly compete for females) and is the reverse of what is seen in the only other pair-bonding modern hominoid, the gibbon. The reproductive-advantage idea is a good story, but it reminds us that we should always be wary of stories that do not fit all the facts. Nevertheless, even though we cannot observe long-extinct hominids in action, it would be unwise for us to forget that their behaviors must have been critical ingredients of their successes and failures.

One particularly intriguing suggestion about the reasons for early bipedality involves the regulation of body and brain temperature in treeless, unshaded environments. In the tropics a major problem once you move away from the forest is the heat load imposed by the strong sun overhead. Shedding this heat is important, particularly for the brain, which can be damaged quickly by overheating. If you stand up, you minimize the heat-absorbing surface area that you present to the sun, even as you maximize the area of your body available to lose heat by radiation and by the evaporation of sweat. And the taller you are, the more you can benefit from the breezes that blow above the level of the surrounding vegetation. In sum, there are plenty of potential benefits from an upright posture on the ground. As to the most important of them, take your pick. But the critical thing to remember is that once you have stood upright, *all* of these potential benefits—and all potential liabilities, too—are yours. The crucial factor is standing up in the first place. And for a newly terrestrial hominoid, the most significant element here was almost certainly having had an ancestor that already favored holding its body upright.

Bipedal though they might have been on the ground, though, these early hominids would hardly have qualified for the epithet "human." In particular, their skulls were still effectively those of apes, housing ape-sized brains in tiny braincases in front of which large faces projected aggressively. This conformation is quite the opposite of that of later hominids, in which we see ever smaller faces that eventually became tucked beneath the fronts of larger, rounder braincases. The long faces of apes have a lot to do with the long tooth rows contained in the upper and lower jaws. Modern apes have quite wide incisor teeth at the front of the mouth, flanked by substantial, pointed canine teeth that project far beyond the level of the other teeth in each tooth row.

This is true of both sexes, but in apes the canines of males are relatively much larger than those of their female counterparts, even in relation to their larger bodies. In animals with large canines there is a gap (known as a diastema) between the side incisor and the canine in the upper jaw. This allows the jaws to close fully, as the lower canines fit into the gaps. Continuing along the tooth row toward the rear, we can see additional distinctions between apes and humans. The lower first premolar of an ape has a single point (cusp); in humans, in contrast, this

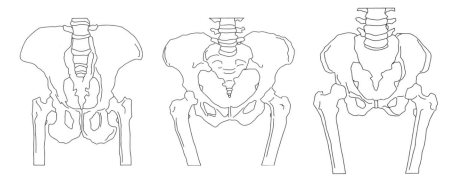

Contrasting shapes in the pelvises of a chimpanzee (left), Australopithecus afarensis *(center), and a modern human (right) show us that on the ground* Australopithecus *was a biped. While different in many details from that of* Homo sapiens *(right), the* Australopithecus *pelvis is broad and flaring like that of the human, and it contrasts strongly with the long, narrow pelvis of the quadrupedal ape.* Courtesy Peter Schmid.

tooth often has two cusps, which is why dentists commonly refer to our premolars as "bicuspids." The three molar teeth behind are relatively elongated in apes, yielding long, parallel-sided tooth rows, quite different from the short, rounded rows of teeth seen in *Homo sapiens*.

Like its body structure, the dentition of *A. afarensis* shows a mixture of similarities to both apes and humans. Presumably, the ape resemblances of *A. afarensis* represent retentions from an ancestral condition that was common to both forms. In particular, the teeth of *A. afarensis* were large, except for the canine. Nonetheless, this tooth still projected somewhat beyond its neighboring teeth, required a small diastema in the upper jaw, and had some of the pointy shape of an ape canine. In addition the enamel covering the teeth was thick, a characteristic of most early hominids, though not of *Homo sapiens*. This is a feature thought to reflect a dietary shift away from soft fruits and toward tougher foods such as tubers.

Despite certain humanlike features, though, many paleoanthropologists like to refer to early hominids such as *A. afarensis* as "bipedal apes." There is plenty of justification for this in terms of the behavioral capacities we may infer for them, for the making of stone tools was still far in the future when *A. afarensis* frequented the African forest edges and woodlands. And there is very little reason to suppose that this species and its like represented any significant cognitive refinement over what we see in the apes today. It's important, though, not to underestimate the mental qualities of the apes—and by extension, of the early hominids. Apes show remarkable, if limited, powers of intuitive reasoning, as well as a striking ability to communicate their emotional states and to understand the motivations of other individuals. They even develop local "cultural" traditions involving the transmission from one generation to the next of learned behaviors such as cracking nuts on stone anvils and "fishing" with sticks in termite mounds. Indeed, many primatologists think that the capacity for culture in this restricted sense is a basic great-ape trait, and if so, we have even greater reason to believe that the apes can give us a general picture of the apparently quite impressive intellectual starting point of our own lineage.

But whether or not this turns out to be the case, it is still important not to view early hominids simply as junior-league versions of ourselves: implicitly, creatures striving to become us. Equally clearly, these ancient relatives did business in their own unique ways and weren't apes, either. But one of the ways in which *A. afarensis* and species like it seem to have been significantly closer to apes than to us was the speed with which they developed from infancy to maturity. Young apes grow up much more quickly than young humans do; a male chimpanzee is reproductively mature at about six to seven years of age, for example, whereas a male human takes twice as long, or longer. This prolonged maturation process—which, it is important to note, extends the period of social learning—expresses itself among other things in the rate at which the permanent teeth erupt. It has been shown that the earliest hominids matured quite rapidly, at rates probably comparable with those of apes. A relatively rapid developmental process may, indeed, have characterized hominids until quite a late stage in their evolution.

Australopithecus afarensis, though a good example of its group, is only the best known of several species that were traditionally classified in the subfamily Australopithecinae of the family Hominidae. This subfamily is nowadays implicitly taken to include all of the extinct hominids, with the exception of those allocated to the genus *Homo*—which raises problems of definition that have yet to be adequately addressed. There is also, inevitably, some argument as to whether this group deserves the status of subfamily; there is, after all, debate even over the level at which Hominidae itself should be recognized. Most scientists thus currently prefer to use the more informal term "australopiths" for this group, and we'll do so here.

The australopiths have been known since 1924, when the first such specimen, described under the name of *Australopithecus africanus*, was found in a lime quarry in South Africa. This specimen consisted of the skull of a very young individual, which immediately introduced problems because young apes and humans resemble each other in skull proportions much more than adults do. What's more, even as an adult this child would have possessed a rather small brain, and at the time paleoanthropology still remained largely under the sway of the large-brained but fraudulent Piltdown specimen. It would be another quarter century before it became generally accepted that the most ancient hominids had not been distinguished from other primates by the big brain we so prize in ourselves today.

Numerous finds in the 1940s and subsequently, however, have demonstrated that the South African australopiths were no mere localized curiosity. Indeed, in the period between about 4 and 1 million years ago at least eight australopith species, all African, are now routinely recognized in the genera *Australopithecus* and *Paranthropus* (though sometimes the genus *Australopithecus* is used to include both). In the welter of new species the long-standing distinction made between the so-called robust australopiths, with relatively heavily built skulls, and the more lightly built graciles is gradually yielding to a recognition that a much more complex branching pattern of descent probably characterized the australopiths during their long tenure on Earth.

There is as yet no consensus view of the relationships among these early hominids. But at the moment many are happy to look upon the 4-million-year-old *A. anamensis* as a "stem" species, which most likely

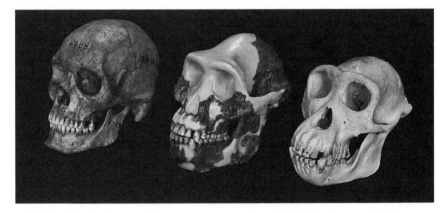

In contrast to the Homo sapiens, *or modern human skull (left), with its balloon-like braincase and tiny face, both the chimpanzee (right) and the* Australopithecus *(center) skulls exhibit small braincases and large, protruding faces.* Photo by K. Mowbray, AMNH.

gave rise fairly directly to our old friend *A. afarensis*, known from between about 4 and 3 million years ago. An approximately 3.5-million-year-old fragment of lower jaw from Chad has been called *A. bahrelghazali*, but many scholars consider this to be a central-western African version of *A. afarensis*. If the distinction between gracile and robust forms is an accurate one, it was shortly before 3 million years ago that the gulf began to develop. *Australopithecus africanus* is the classic example of the gracile forms and is found in sites in central southern Africa that are hard to date but that are believed to fall in the period between a little more than 3 million and a little less than 2 million years ago.

A very recent find of an as-yet incompletely excavated skeleton from very early levels at Sterkfontein, the classic *A. africanus* discovery site, is at least 3.3 million years old and most likely represents a distinct species antecedent to *A. africanus*. From within the time span of *A. africanus* comes the Ethiopian species *Australopithecus garhi*, named in 1999 from a handful of fossils that included an upper jaw with rather large chewing teeth. These fossils mystified their discoverers to such an extent that they left open the question of whether their new species might anticipate *Paranthropus* or *Homo*, or whether it might even be a late version of *A. afarensis*, which seems the most plausible option.

The robust forms are typified by *Paranthropus robustus*, a species from South African sites probably dating to between about 2 and 1.5 million years ago, and by the so-called hyperrobust *Paranthropus boisei* from sites in eastern Africa dating from 2.2 to 1.4 million years ago. All australopiths have large chewing teeth, but those of the robusts are truly massive, with premolars of molar-like proportions. In contrast, there is significant diminution of the incisor and canine teeth, which are tiny. The huge molars rapidly wear flat and are implanted in massive jaws. Most scientists see in these fossils evidence that a group of australopiths departed from the omnivorous ancestral condition and embarked on a lifestyle that involved processing large quantities of tough vegetal foodstuffs or perhaps even invertebrates. The massive chewing apparatus needed to accomplish this dietary shift is accompanied, among other things, by the presence of sagittal cresting, whereby the rear centerline of the braincase is marked by a thin vertical ridge of bone. The robust lineage can be traced back to at least 2.5 million years ago, when the species *Paranthropus aethiopicus* showed up in eastern Africa, and some scientists have even argued that *A. afarensis* shows features foreshadowing the robusts. Unlike the later and evidently more specialized robusts, which had quite flat faces, the earlier *P. aethiopicus* possessed a rather projecting snout and fairly substantial front teeth.

Overall, then, the australopiths were a diverse group indeed. With the exception of the highly specialized later robusts, most of them probably had fairly varied diets, eating pretty much whatever food they could lay hands on, although microscopic examination of the teeth reveals wear surfaces textured rather like those of frugivores or omnivores, and one study of bone chemistry suggests that *A. africanus* was already consuming substantial quantities of meat. Hunting in itself would probably have been nothing new for a hominoid—some chimpanzees hunt from time to time, sometimes quite frequently. These remote precursors of humans probably scavenged most of their animal protein, however, and it is highly unlikely that they ever pursued anything larger than small prey. With the possible exception of the robusts they all probably had broadly similar lifeways. But it is hard to avoid the impression that these various different types of australopiths were busily exploring the options offered by the range of new habitats made available by the climatic changes affecting their continent. We can thus look upon the multiplicity of australopith species as the outcome of a set of evolutionary experiments that was made by a special kind of hominoid learning to cope with new habitats. And it was out of this process of experimentation that the ancestors of our own genus, *Homo,* somehow emerged.

Emergence of the Genus *Homo*

I t is widely assumed that our own genus, *Homo*, arose somewhere among the welter of australopith species. But nobody knows for sure which australopith was closest to our own ancestry. As always, the hunt is on for more fossils; but in the meantime there are several candidates for classification as the earliest known *Homo*.

The first really ancient species of our genus to have been named is *Homo habilis*, described by Louis Leakey and two colleagues in 1964. The fossils—a rather fragmentary bunch consisting of a broken lower jaw, some pieces of braincase, and some hand bones—were found in Olduvai Gorge, a hot, dusty canyon in the Serengeti Plains of what is today Tanzania. Leakey and his wife, the archaeologist Mary Leakey, had been working there for decades, in search of the makers of the crude stone tools that had been found in the oldest rocks exposed on the sides of the gorge. In 1959 they thought they had the remains of an early toolmaker when they found the cranium they named *Zinjanthropus*. But this, alas, was clearly a robust australopith (eventually renamed *Australopithecus boisei*), albeit a splendid example of one. And nobody at the time was willing to regard such early hominids as toolmakers.

It was a great relief for the Leakeys, then, when in 1960 the mandible of a much more lightly built hominid came to light in the very lowest levels of the gorge (known as Bed I). This was followed over the next three years by some other bits and pieces, including a fragmentary cranium from a bit higher up in the rock layers (lower Bed II). Here at last was a hominid that appeared worthy of being a maker of stone tools and the proud bearer of the name *Homo habilis*—"handy man."

Not that everyone agreed. For example, in the corridors of Cambridge University, Leakey's own alma mater, there was at the time much harrumphing over whether there was really enough "morphological space" between the australopiths and the next-known species of *Homo*, *H. erectus*, to admit a new species. Of course, such "space" there was, and in abundance; but those were the days when the influence of the evolutionary synthesis was at its height, and when it was considered sophisticated to recognize as few hominid species as possible. However, what was perhaps most unsettling about Leakey's claims was the extraordinary age of the specimens he was proposing to classify as the first species of *Homo*.

Until the early 1950s, when radiocarbon dating came along, there was no way to determine the age of fossils in years. And even radiocarbon dating was good only back to about 40,000 years ago. Beyond that, it was possible only to say that particular rocks were older or younger than others and to assign them to a place in the worldwide sequence of geological periods. Leakey had himself hazarded the guess early on that his *Zinjanthropus* was 600,000 years old; but although this figure was widely regarded as reasonable, it had been essentially plucked out of the air. Imagine the furor, then, when in 1960 Leakey and two colleagues announced the result of an early application of the new method of potassium-argon dating to the volcanic ashfall rocks of Olduvai Gorge Bed I: they had come up with an age of 1.75 million years! This was almost unimaginably ancient, and although the date has been amply confirmed since, it took a while before it was generally accepted that the toolmaking *Homo habilis* was indeed that old.

Just what did those early stone tools found at the bottom of Olduvai Gorge consist of? When the Leakeys began to find very crude stone tools in East Africa, archaeologists' notions of what very early stone tools should look like was conditioned by the implements that had been found in Europe from the early nineteenth century onward. These were laboriously worked lumps of stone that had been struck with a stone or bone "hammer" on both sides until they assumed a symmetrical shape, most usually that of a teardrop. Louis and Mary Leakey, on the other hand, recognized at Olduvai Gorge that simple small cobbles (fist-sized, river-rounded lumps of rock) with a flake or two chipped off one or both sides by blows from another rock represented the results of deliberate toolmaking. They attributed the stone tools thus produced to an "Oldowan" (from "Olduvai") industry, often referred to, for obvious reasons, as "Mode 1" of artifact making.

Eventually it turned out that the chipped cobbles, though they were often used for pounding, were probably not the primary implements the toolmakers were after. Instead, it was the small, sharp flakes struck from them that were the invaluable cutting utensils the toolmakers desired. It didn't matter exactly what these flakes looked like; it was the existence of their sharp cutting edges that was the important thing.

And why not? The flakes, even if only an inch or two long, were highly efficient cutting implements, especially when made from the best

The hand of a modern toolmaker serves as a scale for replicas he has made of "Oldowan" stone tools, the earliest tools made. In the bottom row are sharp stone flakes; in the upper row are the "cores," mainly river cobbles, from which those flakes were created with a blow from another stone. Courtesy of Kathy Schick and Nicholas Toth, Stone Age Institute.

kinds of stone. Experimental archaeologists have butchered entire elephants using such tools—and rapidly, to boot. Early hominids, chancing on the carcass of a dead antelope or buffalo, could have carved off a limb in no time flat and could then have retreated to a safe place to eat it, something that they could not possibly have contrived without the aid of these cutting tools. And once the entrails were gone and the limbs of the dead animal had been stripped of flesh by scavengers, early hominids could still have used their cobble tools to smash the bones and extract the nutritious marrow that was otherwise only available to animals, such as hyenas, that possessed extremely powerful crushing jaws.

If we assume, as seems reasonable from what we know of chimpanzees, that the ancestors of the first hominid makers of stone tools already had a certain amount of flesh—whether hunted or scavenged—in their diet, stone tools must have made an enormous difference in their lives. Small-bodied scavengers like them would have been highly vulnerable out on the open savanna, especially when competing for carcasses with lions, hyenas, leopards, wild dogs, and other dangerous animals. Any device that would have made it possible for them to carry valuable meat to safer places on cliffs or among the trees would have been an extremely valuable survival mechanism.

What did this new behavior—this chipping of flakes off small cobbles—mean for the cognitive abilities of the early toolmakers? To a modern human this might seem like a pretty rudimentary ability, but in fact it is a highly significant one. Extensive efforts have been made to teach at least one modern ape to make stone tools, by laborious demonstration and example. And this individual—a star in language experiments— failed to get the idea, never learning to hit one stone with another at exactly the right angle needed to chip off a sharp flake. Admittedly, this is not easy. Making stone tools, particularly by using a rock hammer, is difficult and extremely tough on the hands, and it is hard to imagine how the first individual figured out how to do this successfully.

Of course, it is hard or even impossible for us to imagine the cognitive states of any beings that do not mentally process information in the same way we do. But it is particularly tricky to imagine what was going on in the head of the first bipedal ape to deliberately make a stone tool with the outcome clearly in his or her mind. For although this mind held an idea we can readily grasp, it was clearly a mind that was vastly different from our own. What we can be sure of, however, is that this invention ushered in a new set of behavioral possibilities—a range of possibilities that is clearly beyond what is available to any ape now living. And there can be no doubt that the first toolmaking hominids had made a significant leap in the ability to visualize the possibilities offered by the world around them.

For the first toolmakers not only understood the basic mechanics of stoneworking, but they also anticipated needing the tools they would make. Like us, they planned ahead. We know this because they would carry intact cobbles for up to a couple of miles or more before making them into tools as needed. The right kinds of rock for making stone tools are not just lying around on the landscape everywhere; they are found in particular places, which might not be the places where tools would be required. And at some early sites where animals had been butchered, archaeologists have been able to piece together, from the fragments left by the toolmaking process, whole cobbles of rock types not naturally found in the neighborhood.

The only explanation for these cobbles' presence was that the butchering hominids had brought them in. This is ample evidence that the early toolmakers selected suitable raw materials and carried them around in the anticipation of needing tools. Modern chimpanzees hunt small mammals cooperatively, but they normally do so only when the opportunity presents itself spontaneously. Ancient toolmaking hominids evidently armed themselves in anticipation of butchering the carcasses of animals they were intending to hunt or to scavenge. They had foresight. In some rudimentary way, they were planners.

So who were the first makers of stone tools? The *Homo habilis* fossils from Olduvai are only about 1.8 million years old, and archaeologists have now identified several spots on the landscape of eastern Africa where ancient hominids discarded crude stone tools during the period between about 2.5 and 2 million years ago. At some of these places the bones of dismembered animals were also found, but at none of them were there hominid fossils. Perhaps the closest thing is a 2.5-million-year-old site at Bouri, in Ethiopia, where animal bones bearing cut marks have been found not far from australopith fossil fragments that have been identified as belonging to the species *Australopithecus garhi*. Of course this association does not fit well with the "man the toolmaker" model that motivated Louis Leakey to name his new hominid *Homo habilis*. But perhaps it helps to explain why all the potential candidates for first maker of stone tools are only with difficulty shoehorned into a coherent notion of the genus *Homo*.

The hominid fossil record from between 2.5 and 2 million years ago is pretty sparse, but at present it is possible to argue that none of the hominid fossils—all of them fragmentary—that have been reported from this period should really be assigned to the genus that includes our own species *Homo sapiens*. It is even possible to suggest that the Olduvai *Homo habilis* itself does not fit into the genus, despite Leakey's early belief that the cranial fragments indicated a brain somewhat bigger than typical for australopiths.

But however we might want to classify it, it does seem likely that the earliest toolmaker had the bodily proportions of an australopith and was small-bodied and quite small-brained. Evidently, it did not take big brains to make stone tools. And, when you think about it, that's not implausible at all. For any behavioral innovation has to originate with an individual, who must belong to a preexisting species. He or she cannot differ too much from his or her non-toolmaking parents. Innovations of all kinds must arise *within* species, because there is simply no other place they can do so, which is why there is no reason to associate behavioral novelty with the emergence of new species. We cannot use the arrival on the scene of new species to explain new behaviors. And the reverse applies as well—there is no reason to anticipate that new species will invariably demonstrate radically new behaviors. This is certainly the case with the first hominids who demonstrably had body proportions like our own: the first "true" *Homo*.

Clearly, "early *Homo*" as currently conceived would have looked very different from us when moving around on the landscape. The first kind of human whom we might have recognized as in some way "one of us," at least from a distance, is the species often referred to today as *Homo ergaster* (or sometimes as "African *Homo erectus*"). Best known from a miraculously preserved skeleton (often known as the "Turkana Boy") from West Turkana in northern Kenya, here at last is a being constructed essentially like us, at least from the neck down. Such structure is not foreshadowed at all in the hominid fossil record—though fossil postcranial bones are admittedly few and far between and are hard to interpret in isolation.

Indeed, it is vanishingly rare to find even a partial skeleton of the same fossil hominid individual, especially in the more remote past— most of the record—before the innovation of burial, a scant few tens of thousands of years ago. The preservation of the "Turkana Boy" skeleton— technically known by its Kenya National Museum catalog number, KNM-WT 15000 (see the frontispiece of this book)—is the result of an astonishing concatenation of circumstances. When he died, the place where the Turkana Boy was found was probably part of an extensive marsh on the floodplain of an ancient river. Why this lone adolescent should have been there amid the shallow standing waters and grassy, reedy tussocks we shall never know. But for whatever reason, he died and pitched face-down into the swamp, unnoticed by any of the flying, swimming, or running scavengers that would have dismembered and chewed on his body had it lain almost anywhere else. The heavy sediment load of the water, combined with its relative stillness, combined to ensure that the body remained undisturbed and was rapidly covered by the protective sediments in which his bones fossilized. In this way his remains escaped the almost invariable fate of dead individuals on a landscape such as the ancient Turkana Basin: the scattering of body parts and bones, and their complete or partial destruction by scavengers and weather.

This miracle of postmortem survival presents us with one of very few examples from the early human fossil record in which we can see clearly the relationship between the different body parts—most significantly, the skull and limb bones—of a single individual. And these remains show us that *Homo ergaster*, as far as we know unlike any of its contemporaries, had an effectively modern body skeleton. Quite evidently, our lineage did not acquire its unusual tall, striding structure through a gradual process of natural selection over long ages. Instead, the example of the Turkana Boy strongly suggests that we acquired it during a rather short-term episode, probably because of a relatively minor alteration in a regulatory gene that had a cascading effect on structure throughout the body.

Earlier hominids were short in stature, four to five feet tall at most. The Turkana Boy, in contrast, stood about five feet three inches tall when he died at around eight years of age, and it is estimated that he would have topped six feet at maturity. Tall, long-legged, and slender, this individual was clearly suited for life on the open savanna, far away from the shaded forest edges in which it seems his remote forebears had largely been confined. Indeed, his build and body proportions are strikingly similar to those of humans who live in similar tropical environments today, where a main problem is one of losing excess body heat.

It is with such fossils as the Turkana Boy that we can finally be reasonably confident that hominids had lost the luxuriant body hair that the common ancestor of hominids and apes undoubtedly possessed. The reduction to insignificance of most of the hairs covering the body and the proliferation of sweat glands almost certainly went hand in hand, as part of the hominid body's heat-shedding mechanism. We simply don't know how much body hair the early bipeds possessed. Because they seem to have spent most of their lives in at least partial shade, it is likely that they retained some, whereas hominids like the Turkana Boy almost certainly had naked skin. This skin was with equal certainty dark in color, for the highly damaging effects of the rays of the tropical sun are mitigated by an abundance of the dark pigment melanin, which blocks their penetration.

Unsurprisingly, the Turkana Boy does have some bony characteristics that are different from what we find in *Homo sapiens* today. His rib cage, for example, resembles Lucy's in tapering outward quite dramatically from top to bottom, unlike our barrel-shaped torsos; and the central holes in his vertebrae through which his spinal cord passed are rather small. It has been argued that he is thus unlikely to have possessed the fine control of the chest wall that is necessary to modulate air movements in order to produce the sounds of speech. But it is more likely that this narrowness of the vertebral canal was pathological, perhaps even reflecting a condition that contributed to his early death. Still, numerous other details of the Boy's skeleton also differed from what is typical of *Homo sapiens* today. What's more, the strong probability is that, like earlier hominids, the Turkana Boy had developed rather quickly; for although he had lived for only eight short years when he died, his developmental stage was closer to that of a modern human of about eleven.

Above the neck the story is more clearly different from ours. The Turkana Boy had a skull that, although more recognizably like our own than any australopith's, was nonetheless very distinctive. His braincase, for example, was small. It had contained a brain about 880 cubic centimeters in volume, which is close to twice the size of an australopith's but not much more than half the size of an average modern human's. His face projected forward quite markedly: again, much less so than most australopiths', but substantially more than ours; and he possessed chewing teeth of considerable size. The overall appearance of his skull, then, is substantially less modern than that of his body skeleton.

The Turkana Boy is dated to 1.6 million years ago, but other specimens that are also often identified as his species, *Homo ergaster*, date from as long ago as 1.9 million years or even a little more. In terms of cultural innovation this is significant because it means that, for several hundred thousand years after its first appearance, *Homo ergaster* continued to use a stone-tool technology indistinguishable from the one that had been employed by its archaic precursors, essentially since toolmaking began. Unfortunately, there are few archaeological sites for this critical period, and there is no way to associate specific types of stone tools with any particular kind of hominid. But what we see here certainly reinforces the notion that we should not expect that new kinds of hominid will necessarily be accompanied by new kinds of cultural expression such as an improved tool kit.

Of course, stone tools are only the most indirect indicators of behavior, and they occupy their central place in our interpretations of early hominid activity patterns simply because they preserve so extremely well and thus constitute such a high proportion of the total Paleolithic archaeological record. Nonetheless, at the moment we have little reason to conclude that the physically new kind of hominid represented by *Homo ergaster* was at first behaving radically differently from its precursors.

Still, it remains likely that *Homo ergaster* possessed a greater cognitive potential than its predecessors had—a potential that could be put to use by appropriate technological discoveries. And indeed, at about 1.5 million years ago (possibly a bit more), *H. ergaster* began to manufacture an entirely new kind of stone tool. Previous toolmakers had apparently been in search simply of a particular attribute: a sharp cutting edge. They clearly hadn't cared exactly what the flakes they produced looked like; the important thing was that they could be used to cut. But after *H. ergaster* had already been around for a good while, toolmakers, while continuing to produce simple stone-flake tools of the old kind, also began to make larger tools by shaping a piece of stone on both sides into a symmetrical and standard pattern.

This new and labor-intensive kind of tool, the teardrop-shaped "Acheulean handaxe" (from St. Acheul, the locality in France where they were first described), was clearly made according to a mental template that must have existed in the toolmaker's head before the shaping started. Once this new technology had become established, such tools began to be produced in huge numbers. Sometimes, indeed, they were churned out in much greater quantities than you might think would be needed for practical purposes. And although handaxes (and their variants, narrow-pointed picks and straight-edged cleavers) were highly utilitarian (handaxes have been dubbed the "Swiss Army knives of the Paleolithic"), it is hard to avoid the impression that, occasionally at least, the handaxe-makers were simply repeating a somewhat compulsive and stereotyped behavior pattern.

So, just what does this new kind of tool imply about the kind of consciousness possessed by its makers? Clearly, handaxes marked some kind of cognitive leap by those who made them (it's not evident that the very first toolmakers could ever have come up with such tools). But just what this means for the rest of their behavioral repertoire is difficult to know. There is little independent indication, for example, that early Acheuleans were hunting animals any larger or harder to catch than their predecessors had done.

Up to the time of *Homo ergaster*, all members of the hominid family had been confined to Africa. For the period before about 2 million years ago, there are no credible reports of hominid fossils from anywhere else in the world. Once humans with modern body proportions were on the scene, however, it appears not only that they rapidly left the continent of their birth but also that they penetrated all the way to eastern Asia in a remarkably short amount of time. Recent datings, for example, have

A toolmaker holds the replica he has just made of an "Acheulean" handaxe. Stone tools of this kind began to be made in Africa more than 1.5 million years ago and were the first to correspond to a "shape template" that toolmakers held in their minds before they created the tool. Courtesy of Kathy Schick and Nicholas Toth, Stone Age Institute.

placed hominids on the Indonesian island of Java as early as 1.8 to 1.6 million years ago, although the earlier date, in particular, has been contested. Java is an emblematic place in the annals of paleoanthropology, because it is there that the first really ancient hominid remains were discovered, back in the 1890s.

In those days the number of hominid fossils known was very small indeed, and none of them was anywhere near as ancient as the Java material. Inevitably the new form, named *Homo erectus* in recognition of its upright stance, assumed a central role in interpretations of human evolution. Today it seems less likely than it did then that *Homo erectus* represents a mainstream "stage" of human evolution lying between the australopiths and the Neanderthals. Indeed, it is highly probable that this was a local species that evolved in eastern Asia after its ancestor, possibly *Homo ergaster* or something like it, had arrived there. Nonetheless, many authorities still bow to tradition and use the notion of *Homo erectus* to encompass a large variety of hominids from Africa, Asia, and Europe, including those referred to in this book as *Homo ergaster*—a complication of which anyone trying to navigate the literature of human evolution needs to be aware.

Still, removing *Homo erectus* from its central position on the human evolutionary tree certainly doesn't make it any less interesting, for if we accept the early dates, this species had a longer run on Earth than any other hominid species we know of. Most known Javan *Homo erectus* specimens probably date from the period between about 1 million and 700,000 years ago, but one sample of skulls that is usually identified as this species has been dated to as little as 40,000 years ago. And this date, probably not coincidentally, is close to that at which *Homo sapiens* probably first arrived in the Indonesian archipelago. We can thus begin to speculate that our species was implicated in the eventual disappearance of another hominid, *Homo erectus*, that may have endured in its East Asian enclave for more than a million and a half years.

Some rather fragmentary fossils from China, and crude stone tools from the Pakistani site of Riwat that are clearly the work of hominids, have been dated to 1.8 to 1.6 million years ago, as well. But the crown jewels of the early human expansion from Africa are without question the skulls excavated during the late 1990s at the site of Dmanisi, located between the Black and Caspian Seas in the Republic of Georgia. Dated now to around 1.8 million years ago, these exquisitely preserved specimens bear dramatic witness to the early hominid migration out of Africa. Five skulls have now been recovered at Dmanisi. Curiously, they are not all alike; indeed they make an unusually heterogeneous group.

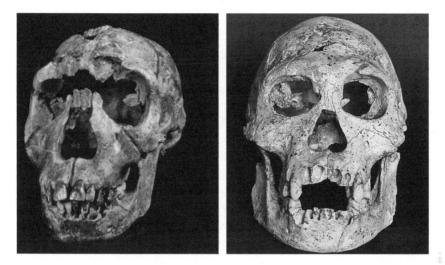

Two crania of early Homo. *On the left is the skull of the 1.6-million-year-old "Turkana Boy" skeleton, generally assigned to the species* Homo ergaster. *Although below the neck this young individual had basically modern body proportions, his head was archaic in many features. His brain was not much more than half the average size of ours today, and his face jutted somewhat in front of a low braincase. On the right is the skull of one of the hominids from the 1.8-million-year-old site of Dmanisi, in the Republic of Georgia. The hominids of Dmanisi provide us with our earliest evidence of hominids outside Africa. They appear to have been small-brained (600–780 cc) and fairly small-bodied, and they possessed only the most rudimentary kind of stone tool.* Photo © Jeffrey Schwartz (left); courtesy of David Lordkipanidze (right).

And none of them is a very close match for any of the hominid crania yet known from Africa for their time period. Still, there is no doubt that the ultimate origin of each of these specimens lay in Africa, and many scholars do believe that this is discernible in their anatomical features.

So what was it that made it possible for hominids to make this first move away from the continent of their birth? The Dmanisi fossils narrow down the range of possibilities. It had been suggested that improved technology was the critical factor that unleashed the mobility of *Homo ergaster* and its like. But, as is clear from an admittedly imperfect record, the invention of handaxe technology, the first intimation we have of technological improvement, came not only long after the arrival on the scene of *Homo ergaster* but long after the diaspora itself. What's more, the stone tools known from Dmanisi are extremely crude, no more sophisticated than the tools associated with *Homo habilis*. So if stone tools are any reflection at all of other aspects of technology that were not preserved, we have to conclude that it was not a newly minted technological prowess that made the expansion from Africa possible. Another suggestion was that it was an increase in brain size and in associated general intelligence that made the difference. Again, though, this notion is not supported by the Dmanisi fossils, which all have rather small brains of 600 to 780 cubic centimeters in volume. This is well below the size of the Turkana Boy's brain, but at the upper end it is similar to some slightly more ancient adult crania from Kenya that may represent his group.

If it was not larger brains or better technology that allowed early hominids to move beyond their natal continent, what was it? It looks as though it must have been their new physical structure. Modern human beings have justifiably been described as "walking machines," odd as that may seem to members of sedentary Western societies. Historically, people all over the world have routinely walked vast distances in pursuit of their normal activities. This is particularly true of hunter-gatherers and nomads. A veteran fossil-hunter who has worked for years in the desertic badlands of Ethiopia tells of his initial amazement that local Afar tribesmen, hearing of the paleoanthropologists' arrival in their area, would walk 25 miles in the blazing heat to say hello and exchange pleasantries for half an hour, then walk 25 miles back again over rough or nonexistent tracks. It is not speed that makes this walking special— far from it, indeed, although a sustained trot serves hunter-gatherers well. Sheer endurance, the ability to keep moving hour after hour, is one of the characteristics that marks humans as a species and as a hunter of an unusual kind.

As far as it is possible to ascertain, all of the "early *Homo*" species probably had archaic (australopith-like) body proportions and retained climbing abilities that would necessarily have compromised their ter-restrial distance walking. Such creatures seem to have been happy to stay, for millions of years, in woodlands and forest edges, with occasional forays into denser forest and more open grassland. And it is surely sig-nificant that it was at the point when the body structure of these archaic forms gave way to the modern anatomy of the Turkana Boy that early hominids moved not only beyond their ancestral habitat but also beyond their ancestral continent, committing themselves to an open-country existence in the process.

Once hominids had emancipated themselves from the forest fringes, they found themselves free to roam more widely than ever before. And they evidently took full advantage of all the possibilities their new con-dition offered. When an organism moves into a new environment, what

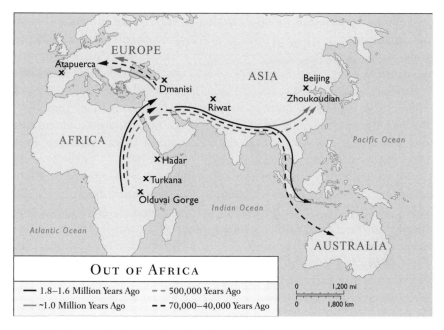

Out of Africa. Early hominids evidently exited their native continent of Africa in several waves. This map shows the most important of these diasporas, the first of which occurred at shortly after 2 million years ago, taking early bipeds as far as the Caucasus (Dmanisi, 1.8 million years old), through central Asia (stone tools at Riwat, 1.6 million years ago) and possibly into southern China and Java as early as 1.8–1.6 million years ago. Archaeological evidence of hominids in Europe by over a million years ago, and hominid fossils at Atapuerca in Spain and Ceprano in Italy by about 900–800,000 years ago, testify to a second wave of emigrants from Africa. A third wave followed the origin of Homo heidelbergensis *in Africa by about 600,000 years ago, spreading rapidly to Europe and also possibly as far as China. Finally,* Homo sapiens *originated in Africa as an anatomically recognizable entity at some point between about 200,000 and 150,000 years ago. By about 80,000 years ago this species had begun to express modern symbolic behaviors, and by around 50,000 years ago it had exited that continent and penetrated east as far as Australia; following a possibly ephemeral occupation of the eastern Mediterranean (without leaving evidence of symbolic cognition) by around 90,000 years ago, it entered Europe at about 40,000 years ago. At this later point it showed the full panoply of modern symbolic consciousness. Adapted from Ian Tattersall, "Out of Africa Again . . . and Again,"* Scientific American, *1997.*

is known as an "adaptive radiation" often ensues, with new species being spawned in different places and exploring all the new ecological possibilities available to them. This certainly seems to have happened in eastern Asia, with the rise there of *Homo erectus*. And it apparently happened in Europe, too, although Europe presented a tougher environment during the Pleistocene. Emigrants from Africa who turned due east would have found themselves able to stay in the subtropical zone for long distances, whereas those continuing north and northeast would soon have encountered major mountain ranges and hostile climatic conditions. Probably it is because of this that although hominid fossils from close to 2 million years ago have been found in tropical Asia and even in the Caucasus, there is no hominid fossil record in central or western Europe before about 800,000 years ago—and few unarguable archaeological traces older than about a million years. And even after that, the record is pretty poor at first.

A site known as the Gran Dolina, in the Atapuerca Hills of northern Spain, has produced some fragmentary early hominid bones, 780,000 years old, that are quite distinctive and have been assigned to the new species *Homo antecessor* ("pioneer man"), although *Homo mauritanicus* ("man of Mauritania") may be a better name for them because they probably belong to the species of that name that was found in North Africa as early as the 1950s. The excavators at the Gran Dolina have suggested that this new hominid might be ancestral both to the Neanderthals on the one hand and to the lineage leading to our species, *Homo sapiens*, on the other. But it is equally likely that these remains represent members of an early and ultimately unsuccessful attempt to colonize the difficult terrain of Europe. The jury is still out on this point, but one undeniably intriguing aspect of the Gran Dolina hominids is that they may have been the victims of cannibalism—and if so, they are the earliest hominids to boast this dubious distinction.

The hominid bones at the Gran Dolina had been broken in exactly the same way as those of other mammals found there that had been butchered and eaten. What's more, hominid and mammal bones alike bear cut marks made by the tools—very crude tools, of the early Mode 1 type—that were used to dismember them. Evidently the animal and human bones were treated in exactly the same way, so the case for cannibalism, though controversial, bears listening to. A possibly slightly older braincase from the site of Ceprano, in Italy, is good evidence for the presence of hominids in another part of southern Europe at about the same time, although the Italian specimen most likely represents a species different from the Atapuerca one: yet another intimation that hominids of this period were vigorously investigating and exploiting the various possibilities that the move out of Africa had presented to them.

When we speak of a migration out of Africa, it is important to avoid giving the impression that expeditions were somehow intentionally sent out to explore the farther reaches of the world. Even more important to remember is that we would be unwise to assume that—because it is the situation we are used to today—the presence of only one hominid on Earth is a normal state of affairs. Rather than suggesting what is normal for hominids in general, it more likely tells us that there is something distinctly unusual about ourselves. Several hominid species at any one time may well have been the norm in Africa in the early days. And even if only some of these species shared the same new physical structure in the period following about 2 million years ago, we can assume that there was at least sporadically some competition among them.

Hominids have probably always been rather thin on the ground, for even in the most favorable of environments, the hunting-gathering lifestyle (how efficient hominid hunting was at this stage is, of course, debatable) requires quite a lot of territory to support each individual. But when a new lifestyle is adopted in a productive new territory (and this would apply to new environments inside Africa as well as to the rest of the world) there will always be a tendency for the population to expand. This tendency will be especially marked at population edges; and even if populations spread outward by only a mile or two a year on average, it would not take very long in geological terms to populate an entire continent. It was thus probably through a slow process of population expansion, rather than through one of deliberate exploration, that Asia, and later Europe, came to be occupied by hominids. Beyond this, such dispersion, occurring as it did in a period of fluctuating environments and geographies, would have been episodic, and local expansions would likely have more often ended in failure than in successful colonization. Indeed, there is evidence that even in relatively recent times the entire ancestral human population went through one or more "bottlenecks," episodes of dramatic reduction in size. We may, in fact, be lucky to be here today.

It is worth noting that this picture fits in well with the idea that there was not just a single hominid diaspora from Africa. Since the rise of *Homo ergaster* first marked the success of the newly mobile modern hominid body, the wanderlust of our kin and ultimately of ourselves has repeatedly asserted itself. It is clear that new and different kinds of hominids have migrated from Africa several times. And indeed, new forms that evolved outside the parent continent may well have come back in later on. What's more, despite the general lack of innovation in stone-tool technologies for a long time both before and after handaxes appeared, it seems that hominids of this period were extremely resourceful and adaptable. For with only a relatively simple tool kit they were often able to persist in the same tract of territory, even as climates fluctuated and resources changed around them.

CHAPTER 5

Getting Brainier

In contrast to the richness of the African fossil record before about 1.5 million years ago, the evidence for later hominid evolution in that continent thins out considerably. This is largely for reasons of geological accident, but it is also because the attentions of rather few paleoanthropologists have been spread out over a continent of vast size, so much of the record presumably remains unexplored. At the same time, for reasons of history as much as of their size and intrinsic importance, the Asian and European records have traditionally loomed larger in the hominid evolutionary story for the period following about 1.5 million years ago. Nonetheless, the logical place to begin our account of the phase of human evolution after the initial move out of Africa is still that continent, where a partial skull was found at the Ethiopian site of Bodo in 1976. This cranium boasts a brain volume of around 1250 cubic centimeters, substantially larger than anything attributed to *Homo ergaster,* and right at the maximum of the range for *Homo erectus.* And in its structure it resembles a species, *Homo heidelbergensis,* that was previously known best from Europe.

In 1908 *Homo heidelbergensis,* "Heidelberg man," was described from a marvelously preserved lower jaw found in a gravel pit near the German village of Mauer, not far from the city after which the species was named. This jaw was unlike anything found before it (only Neanderthals, *Homo erectus,* and various ancient *Homo sapiens* were known at this point), and its discoverer had few qualms in attributing this curious specimen to a new species. The quite robust Mauer jaw possesses a ramus (the part that rises up to the jaw joint) that is notably wide from front to back but is also short from top to bottom. Its corpus (the tooth-bearing portion) is markedly tapered, decreasing in top-to-bottom thickness from front to back.

Later finds revealed that the Mauer specimen is quite unusual in these characteristics; but a whole suite of other features link it with a much better represented group of fossils from the southern French site of Arago. At about 400,000 years old, the latter group is in the same general time range as the best estimate for the Mauer jaw (500,000 years or so). The Arago site yielded not only several lower jaws and part of a pelvis but also an almost complete face with a matching parietal bone, the part forming the top and upper side of the cranium. The Arago cranium in turn recalls a number of other well-preserved skulls from sites around the world. These include not only the Bodo specimen but also crania from Petralona in Greece, Kabwe and Saldanha in southern Africa, and Dali and Jinniushan in China. Regrettably, none of these is well dated, but all do fit plausibly into the period between about 500,000 and 200,000 years ago.

There are certainly differences to be observed among these diverse fossils. For example, the Bodo skull has a large but low-set nasal opening, whereas the Kabwe skull, from what is now Zambia, has a much smaller and higher-set one. In the Bodo and Arago crania the front part of the brain lies much farther forward over the eyes than it does in the Kabwe and Petralona specimens. The shape of the rear of the skull varies somewhat. The eye sockets may be conformed a little differently. And within the whole group there is wide variation in the degree to which the craniofacial sinuses (cavities in the bone structure), and particularly the frontal sinus (the one over the eyes, where you experience "brain freeze" when you swallow a frozen drink too fast), are developed. Yet overall these fossils make a relatively homogeneous group; and for the present, at least, it makes a certain amount of sense to view *Homo heidelbergensis* as a highly successful species, probably of African origin, that became widespread throughout the Old World (Africa plus Europe and Asia).

This species had a brain that was relatively large, although not quite of a size comparable with the modern average. The face is big and projects forward, and it lies beneath distinctive and bulbous brow ridges that are thickest above the middle of each eye socket, and the front surface of which twists upward toward the sides. The lower jaw is long from front to back and bereft of anything resembling a chin. Interestingly, where the base of the skull of *Homo heidelbergensis* is preserved (best seen, perhaps, in the Bodo skull), it shows a distinct downward bend in front of the foramen magnum, the hole through which the spinal cord passes down to the vertebral column from the base of the brain. This is important, for the base of the skull is not only the bottom of the braincase, but it is also the roof of the vocal tract, the space in which we form the sounds that emerge from our mouths as speech.

Language is perhaps the most striking possession of *Homo sapiens* among living creatures; and if we are fully to understand how various unique characteristics of modern human emerged, then it is important to discover when and how our ancestors became capable of speech. For even if the ability to produce the sounds of speech may exist independently of it, language as we know and use it could never have developed independently of the ability to produce speech. The basic vibrations that we manipulate to create the sounds that become speech are produced in our throats, at the vocal cords. But these vibrations are modified higher in the throat, by the muscles that surround the pharynx, a space that loops high above the larynx, or voice box, which contains the vocal cords.

In apes (and in newborn humans), the larynx lies high in the throat, and the skull base is flat. In the resulting short pharynx, sounds cannot be modified much. As the infant human grows, however, the skull base bends and the larynx descends, producing a long pharynx in which a greater variety of sounds can be produced. At least in part, this is a key to the remarkable vocal gymnastics that we perform each time we utter a sentence. Neither apes nor newborn humans can produce the range of sounds necessary for this, and the contour of the base of the skull does seem to be a fairly reliable indicator of the vocal tract's potential for producing the sounds necessary for speech, even though the shortness of the face also plays a role. On the evidence of the bending seen in the base of the Bodo skull, it seems that much of this potential may well have been present in *Homo heidelbergensis*, as long ago as 600,000 years. Still, with the face as yet unretracted to produce balanced proportions of the pharynx and oral cavity, it is doubtful that the full human vocal apparatus was in place in *Homo heidelbergensis,* and there is no other evidence to suggest that these hominids actually spoke.

As with earlier hominid species, the appearance of *Homo heidelbergensis* is not accompanied by any notable change in technological equipment. The sediments from which the Bodo cranium was derived contain mostly Mode 1 artifacts, although Mode 2 tools (handaxes) are also documented in them. Beyond this, though, there is not much to be said at this point about the lifestyle of the Bodo hominid, and we have to turn to Europe for a better behavioral record of *H. heidelbergensis.* And as it happens this record is quite impressive, even though it is mostly limited to a handful of sites in France and Germany.

One of these sites is the cave of Arago in southern France in which were found the various *H. heidelbergensis* fossils that allow us to link the Heidelberg lower jaw to a specimen with a face. At Arago the hominid fossils were mixed in with broken animal bones and crude artifacts of Mode 1 type, and it seems that this site was indeed a place where hominids at least periodically gathered and carried out daily activities, including the butchering of animals. What daily life was like for these hominids, however, is better indicated at the locality of Terra Amata, a little bit to the east of Arago on France's Mediterranean coast. This site, a little bit younger than Arago at about 350,000 years old, is thought to represent a beach camp that was seasonally occupied by Ice Age hunters. Stone tools, animal bones, and ashy sediments attest to the activities of early hominids, and at the site there are also indications of what appear to have been shelters. These, along with similar features at the 350,000-year-old site of Bilzingsleben, in Germany, are the earliest artificial structures on record.

The archaeologists who excavated Terra Amata have reconstructed the best-preserved of the shelters as a hut consisting of an oval saplings implanted in the earth, reinforced around the perimeter with stones, and brought together in the middle to make a roof. Whether or not this structure was covered with animal hides to waterproof it is a matter for conjecture, though the excavators think this was not the case. Just inside the hut, where the ring of reinforcing stones is interrupted for the en-

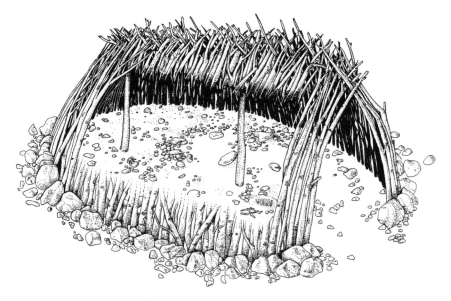

Hut-like structures like these were probably made by Homo heidelbergensis *400,000 years ago. These shelters, built on an ancient beach at Terra Amata, in southern France, were up to 25 feet long. The cutaway reveals an interior containing a circular hearth and stone tools.* Artwork by Diana Salles, after a concept by Henry de Lumley. From Ian Tattersall, *The Last Neanderthal,* 1995.

trance, is a shallow, scooped-out depression containing ash, animal bones, and burned stones, evidence of a hearth where a fire once burned and meat was cooked. This is among the earliest evidence of the domestication of fire, something for which we find consistent evidence only after this time—although a couple of possible instances of hominid use of fire have been reported as early as about 1.6 million years ago, and at one site in Israel fire was consistently used over a long period of occupation some 790,000 years ago.

The stone tools found at Terra Amata are rather more impressive than those from Arago and include crude handaxes and cleavers, as well as flakes of various kinds. Interestingly, Acheulean tools seem to have found their way to Europe rather late—and they barely made it to eastern Asia at all. Before a recent report from China, only the occasional handaxe had ever been found to the east of the Movius Line, a conceptual divide, first noted by the Harvard archaeologist Hallam Movius, that separates eastern and most of southern Asia from the rest of the continent. But once handaxes made it into Europe they became a consistent feature of tool kits, at least locally, until they were supplanted by a new method of toolmaking known as "prepared core." Best known from the Levallois technique, named for the suburb of Paris where examples of it were first found, prepared-core toolmaking involved carefully preparing (shaping with numerous blows) a piece of stone (the "core") in such a way that a single final blow—probably effected by bashing the core on a stone anvil, rather than by striking it with a hammer-stone—could detach from it a thin, light, and effectively finished tool bearing a continuous cutting edge around its periphery.

A whole variety of flakes could be produced in this way, and these could in turn be retouched to various specifications. One of the resulting forms was the flake-based handaxe, generally a smaller tool than the Acheulean handaxe, sometimes itself made on a large flake, but with the same basic shape. Many of the tools manufactured in this way may have been attached to handles, creating compound tools that were much more complex in both concept and potential uses than simple handheld rock implements had been.

It is not easy to judge what this new kind of tool implied about the cognition and lifestyles of the hominids who made them. The underlying technological notion is a great deal more complex than anything involved in simply chipping a piece of stone into a particular shape. So here were hominids (plausibly *Homo heidelbergensis* or something like it) who were capable of quite intricate (though probably intuitive) reasoning, although nothing else in the archaeological record they left behind

An archaeologist holds in his left hand a stone core that he has carefully prepared by shaping it with numerous blows to both sides. In his right hand he holds the sharp flake he has just struck from it with a single final blow. "Prepared-core" toolmaking represented a revolution in stoneworking technology when it was introduced about 300,000 years ago. Courtesy of Kathy Schick and Nicholas Toth, Stone Age Institute.

convincingly suggests that they had the symbolic mental processes and linguistic abilities that we have today. There is also some doubt among archaeologists whether these hominids were clever, guileful hunters along the lines of *Homo sapiens*. Indeed, by the middle 1990s it had become generally believed that hominids of this kind did not have any of the hunting sophistication of historically documented hunting-gathering peoples. However, an extraordinary discovery made in 1995 at the German site of Schoeningen may throw this assumption at least partially into doubt.

Wooden implements preserve very poorly, so they seldom make it into the archaeological record. Normally they rot away within a year or two, or at best within a few millennia, leaving no trace behind. But in a peat bog at Schoeningen, archaeologists discovered not only flint artifacts and cut-marked animal bones but also several miraculously preserved wooden spears dating from about 400,000 years ago, as well as some notched pieces of wood that had probably served as handles for stone-tipped implements. The spears, six to seven feet long, were made from individual spruce saplings, their carefully sharpened tips coming from the bottom of the tree, where the wood is hardest. Each spear was skillfully worked so that its weight, hence the center of balance, was concentrated two-thirds of the way forward. This is exactly the shape of a modern javelin, and it is claimed that these spears were made for throwing and not for thrusting—although their effectiveness as thrown weapons has been questioned. However, their very form does suggest that the hominids who made them may have been equipped for a hunting style that was considerably more sophisticated than many archaeologists had expected.

Before the Schoeningen find, the oldest reasonably complete wooden implement known was a 125,000-year-old spear point found at another German site, Lehringen, lying between the fossilized ribs of a straight-tusked elephant. This more recent spear has been interpreted as a hand-held thrusting implement that would have to have been wielded close-up, a dangerous proposition at best. The Schoeningen hunters, on the other hand, might have hurled their spears at their prey from a safe distance—an enormous improvement in hunting technique.

Once again, we are reminded of—and frustrated by—how indirectly stone tools reflect actual behaviors. Had the Lehringen pachyderm been initially attacked with throwing spears, only finally being dispatched with the thrusted spear? If, as we must suppose, the Lehringen spear was wielded by a Neanderthal, a distinctive group of hominids that occupied Europe and the western part of Asia from some time before about 200,000 years ago until around 30,000 years ago, did the Neanderthals possess only thrusting spears? We can only guess at the answers to questions such as these; but somehow it doesn't seem very likely that after the throwing spear had been invented, putatively well before Neanderthal times, it was promptly forgotten. Indeed, it has been suggested that the very presence of hominids in northern Europe could well have depended on the possession of efficient hunting techniques, because in this area of harsh living conditions large-bodied mammals might have been the only important source of sustenance available to hominids for most of the year.

The stage is thus set for a prolonged debate about the hunting prowess of early Europeans and about how good an indication stone tools are of other aspects of technology, let alone of broader lifestyles. Nonetheless, within the stoneworking domain there is little doubt that the prepared-core technique was explored to its utmost by the Neanderthals.

Homo neanderthalensis was the very first kind of extinct human to be found and thus occupies a very special place in the history of paleoanthropology. In 1856 lime miners emptied a cavity (the Little Feldhofer Cave) in Germany's Neander Valley near Düsseldorf, unearthing part of a hominid skeleton in the process. Its limb bones were humanlike although robust, but it was the skullcap that was really peculiar. For although the brain evidently had been very large (of modern human size), it had been contained within a very distinctive skull vault: long, low, bulging at the rear, and adorned in front with large brow ridges that arched separately over each eye socket.

This discovery was made three years before Charles Darwin published *On the Origin of Species.* In the absence of the idea that these bones might represent an extinct relative of mankind, there was almost no option but to consider that this odd, big-brained skull was that of a strange version of *Homo sapiens,* the only hominid then known on the planet. The apparent possibilities boiled down to two: either these remains were pathological, those of a diseased and deformed individual; or they were the bones of a member of one of the "barbarous" tribes that had formerly occupied Europe (and about whom Roman chroniclers had complained at great length). Almost everyone who entered the initial debate about the Feldhofer specimen took one or the other of these positions. Even the comparative anatomist and evolutionist Thomas Henry Huxley, later known as "Darwin's Bulldog" for his tenacious defense of Darwin's ideas, opted for one of these choices, interpreting the specimen as that of a rather brutish form of modern human. For although in his 1864 book *Evidences as to Man's Place in Nature* he referred to the Neanderthal cranium as the "most pithecoid [ape-like] of known human skulls," he also saw it as being linked to "the highest and best developed of human crania." The sole exception to this chorus was the Irish anatomist William King, who assigned this strange material to its own new species, *Homo neanderthalensis.*

Since 1856, hundreds of fossils comparable with the Feldhofer specimen have been found and given the Neanderthal name. They come from dozens of sites, from Uzbekistan in the east all the way to the Atlantic coast of Europe in the west, and from Wales and Germany in the north down to Gibraltar and Israel on the Mediterranean. All Neanderthals share a distinctive anatomy that is very different from our own; but still the old notion lingers that these hominids somehow represent a bizarre (and by implication inferior) version of *Homo sapiens.* Perhaps, at least today, this is because warm-hearted paleoanthropologists find it somehow discriminatory to exclude a large-brained hominid such as *H. neanderthalensis* from the "privilege" of belonging to *H. sapiens*. But it bears repeating that if morphology means anything at all in our assessment of fossils (and if it doesn't, what are we left with?), the Neanderthals were an evolutionary entity entirely separate from us. And they thus need to be understood on their own terms, not ours, and to be accorded their own separate identity.

Since the middle of the twentieth century it has frequently been claimed that Neanderthals were ancestors of *Homo sapiens* because various late Neanderthal fossils show "advanced" features and various early modern specimens show "primitive" ones. Such claims do not, however, stand up to close scrutiny. The fallback position from this is that Neanderthals and modern humans, belonging to the same species, interbred when they came into contact with each other; but again, the evidence in favor of this is scant at best. In 1999 it was claimed that the skeleton of a young child found at the Portuguese site of Lagar Velho represents a descendant of an intermixed Neanderthal/modern population. However, the anatomical evidence for this imaginative interpretation has been fairly described as "at best ambiguous"; in addition, this child died just 24,500 years ago, long after the Neanderthals were extinct. William King may have based his claim for *Homo neanderthalensis* as a distinct species principally on the rather dubious grounds of his intuition that "the thoughts and desires that once dwelled within [the Feldhofer skull] never soared beyond those of a brute," but there can be little doubt that his resulting classification was entirely correct.

Homo neanderthalensis is by far the best-documented of all extinct hominid species. And it is clear that, just as modern humans do today, individual Neanderthals (and populations from different times and places) differed from each other in their bony structure. Some had lower skull vaults than others, for example, or the bridges of their noses projected more or less horizontally. Some had retreating jawlines; others had more vertical ones. But equally clearly, these variations were on a different theme than ours. They do not simply represent various extremes of the *Homo sapiens* spectrum. Aside from such variations, all Neanderthals had large brains (about 1,200 to 1,740 cubic centimeters in volume; ours range between 1,000 and 2,000 cubic centimeters). And these brains were enclosed in relatively long and flattish skull vaults bearing low foreheads behind distinctive double-arched brow ridges. In profile, you can see that these ridges are smoothly curved as they rise from the roofs of the eye sockets and flow to the frontal bone behind.

In all of these respects the Neanderthal skull contrasts with that of *Homo sapiens*, in which the cranial profile is high and rounded, the dome rising directly above generally small brow ridges that are divided above each eye into distinct central and lateral portions separated by an oblique groove—which you can easily feel above your own orbits. Whereas the rear of the *H. sapiens* skull, as seen from the side, is commonly smoothly curved, that of *H. neanderthalensis* tends to protrude, sometimes in a distinct "bun." High up at the back of the skull, in the midline, there is a curious area of pitted bone, called a suprainiac fossa, which modern humans lack. Seen from the back, the braincase of Neanderthals is smoothly rounded on the sides, rather than having rather vertical side walls as ours does. Unlike the face of modern humans, which is small and tucked beneath the front of the braincase, the Neanderthal face protrudes forward in the midline and is swept back at the sides, with sharply receding cheekbones. The area between the eyes and the mouth is puffed out by large sinuses. The Neanderthal nose is huge, and just within its opening lie some sideways-pointing structures unknown in humans (or in any other primates, for that matter) that are called medial projections and may reflect an unusual configuration of the respiratory system.

The lower jaw may or may not have minor swellings in the midline, but no Neanderthal known has anything like the specialized structure of the human chin. There are even substantial differences in the morphology of the teeth. This list of distinctions between *H. neanderthalensis* and *H. sapiens* skulls could go on and on, but the point should already be clear: Neanderthals and modern humans are exceedingly different in the way they are structured from the neck up.

How about from the neck down? Same story. Although *H. neanderthalensis* was built along the same basic plan as *H. sapiens*, it nonetheless showed numerous differences from us. Some of those differences are, indeed, striking. The Neanderthal pelvis, for example, is broad, flaring widely to the sides. The collarbones are very long, and the rib cage, narrow at the top, broadens greatly to the bottom. There is hardly any waist where the wide lower part of the rib cage meets the flaring pelvis. The limb bones are very thick-walled. They tend to be bowed out somewhat and have very large joint surfaces at their ends that swell out noticeably from the shafts. Again, there is much more detail that could be mentioned, but the bottom line is that the Neanderthals would have presented a very different figure than modern humans do. This would have included the way they moved, for the peculiarities of the Neanderthals' pelvis and torso would have affected their gait, too. Early modern humans arriving for the first time on the Neanderthals' territory

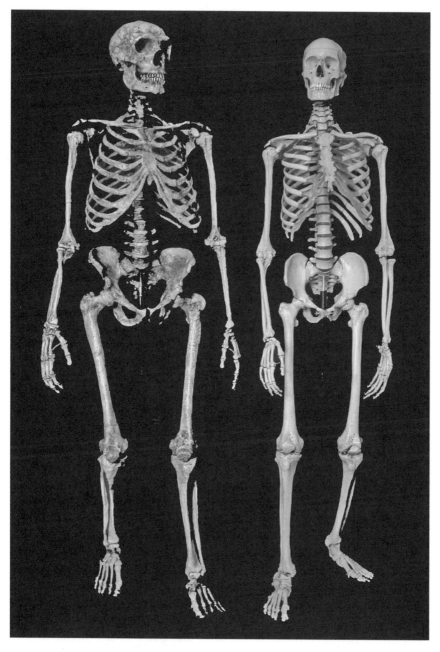

A reconstructed Neanderthal skeleton (left), as compared with a modern human, reveals the Neanderthal's tapering rib cage and wide, flaring pelvis, among many other differences. Although the brains of both individuals were around the same size, they were enclosed in cranial vaults of very different shape, and the faces of both were strikingly different in size and structure. Photo by K. Mowbray, AMNH.

were probably impressed by the "so near yet so far" appearance of these obviously related but equally obviously different hominids.

Just how closely related are the Neanderthals to *Homo sapiens*? Paleoanthropologists have tended not to look too closely at this question, often preferring either to look upon these hominids as a form simply en route to ourselves or as an extreme variant of *Homo sapiens* as we know it. But if we recognize a separate species *Homo neanderthalensis*, then we have to ask ourselves where this distinctive hominid type came from. And we can seek the answer in the fact that the Neanderthals did not exist in isolation. The earliest Neanderthal fossils we know are dated to perhaps as much as 200,000 to 250,000 years ago; but they are rare, and the Neanderthal record becomes relatively good only when we approach more recent times. Still, a scattering of hominid fossils is known from Europe from the period between the appearance of *Homo heidelbergensis*, about 500,000 years ago, and the time at which the first Neanderthals appear.

Interestingly, the fossils from this temporally intermediate era all have a certain number of the features that we associate with Neanderthals—but not all of them. It seems, in fact, that the Neanderthals were part of a larger group of hominid species that diversified in Europe subsequent to the appearance there of *Homo heidelbergensis* or perhaps even of *Homo antecessor*. This is a classic example of the "adaptive radiation" that typically happens when a new kind of animal successfully invades a new territory—as western Europe was to hominids. Once again we see that local diversification has been a major element in the evolutionary history of hominids, as in those of so many other kinds of animal.

The prime example here, perhaps, is a 225,000-year-old cranium found in Steinheim, Germany, in 1933. Despite having been somewhat distorted after burial, this specimen resembles the Neanderthals in, among other things, its brow shape, its large nasal opening, the shape of its eye sockets, its (small) suprainiac fossa, and a hint of medial projections in the nose. But it differs, again among other things, in being relatively small-brained and in lacking the rounded braincase walls and facial puffiness seen in Neanderthals. Many have thus perceived "pre-Neanderthal" features in this specimen, though it is rare to argue that it is actually a Neanderthal. The best interpretation seems to be that the Steinheim cranium represents a species that had recently shared an ancestor with the Neanderthals yet also belonged to its own separate species.

Another example of diversification is provided by the amazing series of hominid fossils, around 500,000 years old, that have been found in

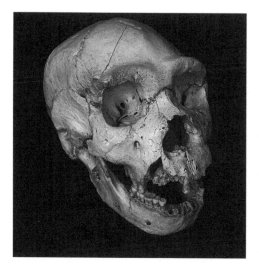

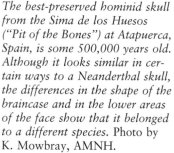

The best-preserved hominid skull from the Sima de los Huesos ("Pit of the Bones") at Atapuerca, Spain, is some 500,000 years old. Although it looks similar in certain ways to a Neanderthal skull, the differences in the shape of the braincase and in the lower areas of the face show that it belonged to a different species. Photo by K. Mowbray, AMNH.

the extraordinary "Pit of the Bones" at Atapuerca in Spain. Here, at the bottom of a deep shaft opening inside a large cave, the broken remains of at least twenty-eight individuals have been found. These hominids are quite distinctive in their own right but have brow ridges, large noses, and other features that are Neanderthal-like. At the same time they lack medial projections, puffed-out faces, and the special features of the rear of the skull that characterize Neanderthals. Yet other European fossils, contemporaneous with those from the Pit of the Bones, share none of their Neanderthal-like features. In this larger context the Neanderthals, rather than seeming to be part of an isolated hominid lineage in Europe, start to fit quite comfortably into a routine scenario of evolutionary experimentation following the first successful hominid incursion into Europe. For whatever reasons, it was the Neanderthals who emerged triumphant from this process of diversification. And this suggests that their related rivals might have suffered, at the Neanderthals' hands, the same kind of fate that awaited the Neanderthals themselves when *Homo sapiens* finally arrived on the European scene.

The notion that the Neanderthals were part of a radiation of hominids in Europe that was separate from the radiation in Africa that gave rise to *Homo sapiens* fits nicely with exciting new information that is becoming available from the molecular record. In the last few years, molecular biologists have succeeded in extracting fragments of mitochondrial DNA (mtDNA) from a few late Neanderthal bones, with instructive results. Mitochondrial DNA is not the same as the nuclear DNA that resides in the nuclei of the body's cells and makes up the chromosomes. Rather, while remaining within the cell's outer membrane, mtDNA resides outside the nucleus in a cellular organelle called the mitochondrion, which is often described as the "powerhouse" of the cell because it is central to the extraction of the energy contained in nutrients.

Mitochondria have their own DNA because the complex cells of which our bodies are built were originally formed a couple of billion years ago by the "capture" of one kind of simple single-celled organism—the ancestor of mitochondria—by another, the progenitor of the rest of the cell. This symbiosis of components from two different lineages of organisms turned out to be highly advantageous, for these complex cells burn fuel up to twenty times more efficiently than other types of cells. Scientists who study the biological histories of modern human populations find mtDNA especially interesting for two reasons. First, it accumulates changes (mutations) much faster than nuclear DNA does, which means that very recent evolutionary events can be detected. Second, it is transmitted exclusively through the mother, because eggs contain mitochondria but sperm do not. This means that the mtDNA gets passed along intact from one generation to the next rather than being reshuffled, as nuclear DNA is, when the genomes of the two parents are combined. As a result, all changes in this type of DNA must be the result of mutations, and mtDNA can thus be used quite simply to trace ancestries through the female lineage within species, as well as to make comparisons among species.

By comparing a short stretch of mtDNA extracted from the original (Feldhofer Cave) Neanderthal specimen with samples obtained from apes and from a variety of modern humans from around the world, investigators arrived at a number of conclusions. First, the DNA sequence that was obtained from the Neanderthal specimen was quite distinct from those of all the modern humans sampled, although it was closer to them than to apes. It showed 27 differences from us, compared with the average of 8 differences that separate members of modern human populations from different areas of the world—and to the 55 that distinguish the average *Homo sapiens* from a chimpanzee. What's more, although the Neanderthal sampled had lived in Europe, its mtDNA was no more similar to that of modern Europeans than to that of any other modern population. Clearly, the Neanderthal specimen was strongly distinguished from all lineages of modern humans and showed no closer resemblances to Europeans of the kind that would have been expected if ancestral European humans and Neanderthals had interbred.

None of this proves conclusively that Neanderthals belonged to the separate species *Homo neanderthalensis,* but it all does point very strongly in that direction. From the mtDNA differences they observed, the investigators calculated a tree of relatedness among the various modern human populations that had been sampled. This analysis indicated an African origin for the modern human gene pool. The scientists also used their data to derive a date for the last common ancestor of Neanderthals and modern humans, which they calculated had lived between 690,000 and 550,000 years ago. This fits pretty well with what we know from the fossil record, since although recognizable Neanderthals only began to show up about 200,000 years ago, the larger grouping to which they belonged had much deeper roots than that. Subsequent to the analysis of the Feldhofer DNA, mtDNA has been extracted from several other Neanderthal specimens with generally similar results (though they do show expected variation among individuals), demonstrating that the initial Feldhofer findings were not just a flash in the pan.

Nobody knows what kinds of groups the Neanderthals lived in, although from the sizes of the sites at which their physical and archaeological remains have been found it seems that social units were typically fairly small, possibly consisting of no more than 15 to 30 individuals of both sexes and all ages. Small bands like this roamed over vast tracts of the sparsely populated landscape, camping in one place for short periods until the local resources were exhausted, then moving on. What those resources were would have varied from time to time with changing climates, and from place to place as groups moved from valley to upland and back again. It has been pointed out that, in contrast to the tropics where plant resources would have been relatively consistent year-round, in Ice Age Europe plant foods that could sustain hominids would have been relatively scarce and more affected by seasonal change.

For this reason, many archaeologists are coming around to the view that meat formed a very important component of the Neanderthals' diet. This again implies that their hunting techniques may have been quite advanced—something that apparently also may be implicit in those spears from Schoeningen. The picture of Neanderthals as predominantly meat-eaters is also supported by the few studies that have been done of the way Neanderthal teeth wore and of the chemistry of their bones (indeed, one study suggested that the Neanderthal examined had been a specialized hunter of extremely large-bodied mammals such as woolly rhino and mammoth). Additionally, frequent close encounters with unfriendly animals may account for the claim that the pattern of fractured and healed bones in Neanderthal skeletons resembles that among rodeo riders today. On the other hand, the only modern humans who historically depended primarily on animal proteins and fats possessed technologies that were highly specialized for obtaining these foods, something not evident in the Neanderthal toolkit.

What is possibly more important about the Neanderthals than their specializations, however, was their considerable adaptability. They survived numerous climatic changes over a huge span of time in a vast and topographically varied area. They could not have been so successful if their behavior patterns had not been highly flexible; and indeed, the evidence strongly suggests that this was the case. In one Italian locale archaeologists excavated some cave deposits with evidence of Neanderthal occupation that dated from 120,000 years ago, when the climate was relatively warm, and others from 50,000 to 40,000 years ago, when conditions were much colder. At the earlier time, occupations seem to have been quite brief, and animal remains were mostly skulls of old individuals. These observations were interpreted to suggest that the Neanderthals had scavenged what remained of the carcasses of aged animals who had died natural deaths. During the more recent period, remains consisted of many different body parts from animals in their prime, and the interpretation is that the Neanderthals had employed ambush-hunting techniques to obtain entire carcasses, during longer stays in the neighborhood. These conclusions are entirely reasonable, but it is impossible to say whether the differences are due to an improvement in hunting techniques over time or whether they simply reflect responses to changing conditions.

The social organization of Neanderthals remains a mystery, although a study at one French site did lead to the suggestion that males and females may have led largely separate lives. But the truth is, we simply do not know. The Neanderthals controlled fire, as their predecessors had for some time, but most evidence for this comes not from deliberately constructed hearths lined with stones but from simple ash deposits. And even where hearths were made, we can be pretty sure that Neanderthals did not sing songs and tell each other stories around them, because it's a good bet that they didn't have language. Language is a symbolic activity, and the Neanderthals left behind no symbolic artifacts (engravings, notations, figurines, and so forth) of the kind that were so typical of their successors, the Cro-Magnons. Cro-Magnon is the name we give to the first *Homo sapiens* who occupied Europe; they are named after the site in southwestern France, "Magnon's Shelter," at which their remains were first found. Nonetheless, there can be little doubt that Neanderthals possessed some form of quite sophisticated vocal communication, presumably supplemented with an extensive repertoire of gestures. And, significantly, at some time before 50,000 years ago the Neanderthals invented the tradition of burying their dead. Neanderthal burial, however, was both occasional and very simple, without the grave goods and other paraphernalia so characteristic of later Cro-Magnon burials (though these apparently did not begin until well after the first Cro-Magnon incursions into Europe).

Of course, deliberate interment of the dead almost certainly did not mean to the Neanderthals what it means to most modern humans, with its overtones of spirituality and future life; but it does suggest some kind of empathy with the deceased. And at the Iraqi site of Shanidar the remains of an individual who survived to an advanced age (maybe 40 years) despite being severely handicapped by a useless arm, perhaps since birth, suggests that such individuals received the long-term support of their groups. Recent studies at other sites have reached similar conclusions. There are many different ways of being hominid, and almost certainly the Neanderthals' way was not ours. But it is nonetheless evident that the Neanderthals were complex beings, who perceived and interacted with the world around them in their own characteristic and sophisticated ways.

The record of hominid evolution in the later Ice Age is better in Europe and the eastern shores of the Mediterranean (the Levant, specifically Israel) than it is in the rest of the world. *Homo heidelbergensis* fossils are known from various sites in southern Africa and eastern Asia following Bodo times some 600,000 years ago, but most of them have not been definitively dated, and none is accompanied by anything like the evidence of lifestyles we have available from France and Germany. In eastern Asia *H. erectus*, or something like it, seems to have survived on the island of Java until as late as around 40,000 years ago, the time at which we can surmise that *H. sapiens* arrived there. In mainland China, on the other hand, *H. erectus* seems to have been replaced by *H. heidelbergensis* or an equivalent well before *H. sapiens* showed up. In Africa, apart from the Bodo specimen, *H. heidelbergensis* is not well dated. However, *H. heidelbergensis* seems to have been broadly succeeded by a rather heterogeneous assortment of hominids represented by crania found in locations as far-flung as Florisbad in South Africa, Ngaloba in Tanzania, and Guomde in Kenya.

To minimize the number of species names while also acknowledging the many ways in which they differ from our living species, many paleoanthropologists have been in the habit of lumping together specimens such as these under the designation "archaic *Homo sapiens*." However, this is a category of convenience more than anything else, and it has had the unfortunate effect of disguising a much more complex underlying pattern of descent than the linear one the "archaic" designation implies. As a result, it is still unclear what the actual pattern was, which is a pity because it was almost certainly among African hominids in this general time frame that true *Homo sapiens* eventually emerged.

On the technological front, it was almost certainly also in Africa that prepared-core tool technology was originally invented; and it is in that continent, too, that long, slender blade tools such as those made by Cro-Magnons appear to have first been made, well over a quarter-million years ago. Of course it is important to bear in mind, when thinking about technologies, that the story of technological development and innovation has been no more linear than that of the hominids themselves. New inventions have appeared, faded, and been replaced by apparently more archaic forms, only to reappear at later times. Indeed, our cultural evolution has very likely been even more complex and tortuous than hominid physical evolution—which is something that we should probably expect, given that cultural traditions can be transferred sideways among contemporaries as well as being transmitted down from one generation to the next.

Modern Human Origins

H *omo sapiens* is an unusual species in many ways. One of those
ways concerns its intricate population history, the result of an
extremely rapid initial spread combined with unparalleled subsequent mobility. Today, thanks to the extraordinary ecological adaptability conferred on it by its ability to respond technologically to the
demands of new environments, *H. sapiens* occupies virtually every in-
habitable region of the world, in huge numbers. But at times during the
climatic rigors of the ice ages, the population of our species (doubtless
like that of its precursors) seems to have been extremely reduced and
fragmented, thus experiencing conditions ideally suited to local adaptation and evolutionary innovation.

A history of this kind is strongly indicated by analysis of human
mitochondrial DNA (mtDNA) sampled from communities around the
world. Amazingly, the total amount of variation in mtDNA found among
the billions of humans worldwide is less than is found among local populations of chimpanzees in Africa. This strongly implies that the ancestral human population passed not very long ago through a bottleneck
in which it was reduced to a few thousand, or perhaps even only a few
hundred, members. From this tiny population, *Homo sapiens* expanded
rather rapidly into the colossus that dominates the world today, ad-
justing, as you would expect, to local conditions in each newly colonized
area of its expanding range. It is for this reason that we are broadly able
to recognize distinctive major geographical variants of our species: Africans, Asians, Europeans, and so forth.

But when we look more closely, the apparent dividing lines disappear. For although local divergence among populations is a common
feature of all successful and widespread species, local variations within
any species always remain essentially temporary distinctions until speciation occurs and separates them into biologically independent entities.
As long as they remain members of the same species, as *Homo sapiens*
despite its variety has so clearly done, all local populations retain the ability to blend and lose their distinctiveness when they come into contact

with each other. And since the end of the last Ice Age, it is this process of fusion that has predominated among human populations. This is why it is so futile to try to classify today's human beings into "racial" groups. Yes, during our species' initial geographic expansion, local populations of *Homo sapiens* in different parts of the world predictably developed distinctive local features, as a result of routine genetic processes going on within them. But for the past 10,000 to 15,000 years or so, the biological history of those populations has principally involved their coalescence, with distinctive features gradually becoming more blurred in a process that has been going on for millennia and that is accelerating today as human mobility increases.

The upshot is that nowadays, certainly from a biological perspective, there are few endeavors more useless than trying to classify the variants of *Homo sapiens*. For by their very nature, local variants within species have no permanence and hence are intrinsically impossible to classify. Nevertheless, tracing the population histories of the various geographical groups of *Homo sapiens* is a subject of wide interest. And it is certainly of importance to know exactly how, when, and where our extraordinary species emerged. In this quest mtDNA has turned out to be especially useful.

Mitochondrial DNA makes evolutionary change in populations relatively easy to follow because it accumulates mutations quickly and, unlike nuclear DNA, is not reshuffled in every generation as genes from each parent are mixed together; mtDNA passes down solely through females, because the male parent's sperm does not contain mtDNA. For a couple of decades investigators have been looking at samples of mtDNA from human groups around the world and comparing the differences among them. A classic study in 1987 arrived at two striking and compatible findings. The first of these was that the variation in mtDNA was highest among African groups, suggesting that diversification had been going on in that continent for longer than it had elsewhere. Indeed, it was possible to interpret samples from the entire remainder of the world as deriving from a single subset of African origin. The second conclusion was that the mtDNA of all modern people is derived from a single female haplotype (variant) that arose in Africa some time between 290,000 and 140,000 years ago.

Because of the inevitable loss of some mtDNA lines (for example, among women who bear only sons) this does not mean that the functionally much more important nuclear DNA of all of us descends from that of a single individual or couple. But the notion of an "African Eve" caught the public imagination. Naturally enough, that initial study was attacked on a variety of grounds, but nonetheless subsequent research broadly supported its conclusions. And different groups of investigators are converging on the notion of an African ancestry for *Homo sapiens* originating not much more than 150,000 to 200,000 years ago.

Thus it seems that our now-ubiquitous species expanded from a tiny population that most likely lived in Africa after about 200,000 years ago, its wanderings subject to the vagaries of climate, environment, and competing species, not least among which would have been other species of *Homo*. First this population spread (a better term than "moved," because the main mechanism involved was almost certainly simple population expansion rather than active expeditioneering) out of Africa, then throughout the Eurasian landmass and into Australasia, and finally into the New World and the Pacific islands. This proliferation was almost certainly not a uniform thing that happened consistently and evenly in all directions; instead, it must have happened sporadically when opportunities presented themselves, with frequent false starts, mini-isolations, and reintegrations of split-up groups. The striking (though superficial) physical variety of humankind today reflects this checkered past.

During this history of spread, local populations developed various physical as well as linguistic and other cultural differences. Some of these physical variations must have been controlled by environments, others by purely random factors. It is clear, for example, that variations in skin color are by and large responses to variations in ambient ultraviolet radiation. The dark pigment melanin protects against the highly damaging effects of ultraviolet (UV) radiation, and the darkest skins occur at low latitudes, where such radiation is strongest. In contrast, farther from the equator complexions tend to be paler, allowing the scarcer UV radiation to penetrate the skin and promote the synthesis of necessary substances such as vitamin D. Similarly, populations living in hot, dry areas tend to be taller and more slender than those living in very cold climates, plausibly because they need to lose heat rather than to retain it as a rounder body shape does. On the other hand, nobody knows why some populations have thinner lips or narrower noses than others, or why many Asians have an additional fold of skin above their eyelids. These inconsequential variations are, indeed, likely to be just the results of random chance.

Various interpretations of the mtDNA evidence yield a range of stories for the spread of *Homo sapiens* around the world. One example roots the *Homo sapiens* family tree in Africa a little less than 150,000 years ago. It identifies four descendant mtDNA lineages (known as A, B, C, and D) among Native Americans. These four lineages are also present in the ancestral continent of Asia, as are lineages designated E, F, G, and M. Europeans show a different set of lineages, called H, I, J, K, and T

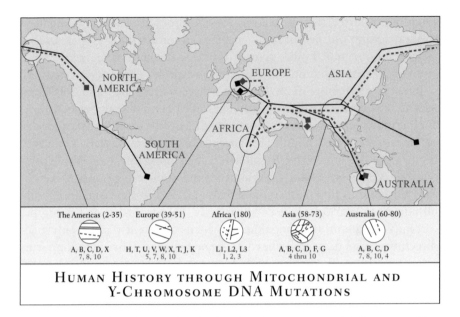

HUMAN HISTORY THROUGH MITOCHONDRIAL AND Y-CHROMOSOME DNA MUTATIONS

Human History through Mitochondrial and Y-chromosome DNA Mutations. Map of the world showing the major routes of human migration as deduced from mitochondrial DNA (solid lines) and Y chromosomal DNA (dotted lines). The actual routes are much more complex than depicted in this figure. To demonstrate the potential complexity, the circles indicate important geographic areas where the branchings of lineages are shown magnified in the larger circles below. The mitochondrial lineages for each geographic region are indicated by letters below the magnified circles. The Y chromosomal lineages for each geographic region are indicated by numbers below the magnified circles. mtDNA haplotype (variant) X is most likely a European haplotype and is also found in the Americas. The numbers in parentheses refer to possible times that the lineages entered the specified areas, in thousands of years. From Rob DeSalle and Ian Tattersall, Human Origins: From Bones to Genomes, *2007.*

through X. Africans present one principal lineage, called L, with three major variants. It is one of these (known as L3) that seems to have been the founder of both the Asian and European groupings. From the differences in mtDNA sequences that have accumulated among the lineages, it is calculated that the L3 emigrants reached Europe between about 39,000 and 51,000 years ago, a date that is in agreement with the archaeological record. However, there are also some apparent anomalies in these data—for example, the rare European mtDNA pattern called X has also been identified in some northern Native Americans. This cannot be explained by recent intermarriage, as this North America X lineage appears to have originated in America in pre-Columbian times.

Despite the complexities, the mtDNA evidence all points toward the same general pattern of human spread. Further supporting evidence comes from examining the human Y chromosome. In terms of the way in which it is inherited, this is the male equivalent of mtDNA, because only males possess it (males have an X and a Y chromosome, whereas females have two X chromosomes). A study of Y chromosomes has produced a family tree of modern human populations that, just like the mtDNA analysis, roots *Homo sapiens* in Africa on the basis of the genetic diversity found there. However, this study also found a larger number of differentiated lineages of Y-chromosome types in Asia than in Africa (in contrast to the greatest differentiation of mtDNA in Africa); and the data further suggested that Africa, the Americas, and East Asia were each outliers relative to the rest of the world, which formed a closer cluster. These are early days for genetic studies, though; and as more populations are examined we will get an increasingly detailed picture of human population movements and integrations around the world from the newly available genetic data.

An African origin for *Homo sapiens* is also suggested by the fossil record, which is unfortunately quite sparse outside Europe for the couple of hundred thousand years that preceded the end of the Ice Age. Still, some paleoanthropologists continue to favor a theory of "regional continuity" in human evolution. This holds that, even though *Homo sapiens* populations have steadily evolved their own local peculiarities over very long stretches of time, major geographic variants have contrived to remain one single species by interbreeding occasionally in the areas where they meet. According to this theory, modern Australian aborigines, for example, are descended from "Java Man" (also known as "Javanese *H. erectus*"), whereas modern Chinese are descended from "Peking Man" ("Choukoutien *H. erectus*").

Supporters of the regional continuity idea have realized the logical impossibility that two distinct variants of the same species, *Homo sapiens*, could be independently derived from the single antecedent species *Homo erectus*. They have thus resorted to including all hominids subsequent to *Homo habilis* in the species *Homo sapiens*. If this tactical device is correct, it would make a mockery of any attempt to sort out hominid evolutionary history on the basis of morphology. In fact, it is tough to defend it either in theory or in practice. Essentially, it is a fallback position from the discredited old "single-species hypothesis," which stated that because human culture so greatly increased the range of ecological niches that hominids could occupy, no more than one kind of hominid could ever in principle have existed at a given point in time.

This fit in with the ideas of the Evolutionary Synthesis as they were absorbed into paleoanthropology during the 1950s, when the hominid fossil record was still quite sparse. But the spectacular enlargement of the record since that time has made such notions entirely untenable, by demonstrating a much greater complexity of events in human evolution.

In eastern Asia *Homo erectus*, or a species close to it, had persisted into the period that saw the abrupt arrival of *Homo sapiens* in the area. A similar scenario played out with *Homo neanderthalensis* in Europe and western Asia. The Americas, however, were not colonized by hominids until long after *Homo sapiens* had become a recognizable species, and perhaps only as recently as 15,000 years ago. Thus, if only by elimination, we have to look to Africa for the emergence of our own species. And how we interpret the relevant African fossil record has been considerably confused by the general acceptance of the category "archaic *Homo sapiens*," into which a rather motley assortment of fossils has been placed.

The species to which we belong today is actually quite clearly defined by such skeletal features as its very distinctively shaped brow, chin, and thorax. Yet, under the sway of the linear thinking induced by the Evolutionary Synthesis, paleoanthropologists have been ready to include in this species virtually any fossil from the past 200,000 or 300,000 years that possessed a reasonably large brain. Even the highly distinctive Neanderthals have been included within *Homo sapiens*, although fortunately all along we have had a vernacular name available to distinguish them. But for African fossils we don't have any readily accepted name of this kind, and this has helped blur the physical boundaries of our species to an extent that has thoroughly obscured its origins.

One result of this has been that a number of clearly non–*Homo sapiens* specimens, from places such as South Africa's Florisbad and Tanzania's Ndutu and Ngaloba, have been filed away as "archaic *Homo sapiens*" and effectively forgotten. As a result, we are glimpsing only indirectly—if at all—many interesting things that were happening among African hominids between about 200,000 and 100,000 years ago. Nevertheless, it is clear that hominids of this period include the first intimations of the emergence of modern anatomy.

Perhaps the best evidence for the early presence in Africa of hominids that looked pretty much like modern humans comes from a skull recovered at the site of Herto, in Ethiopia, that may date to as much as 160,000 years ago. From the description published by its discoverers it is not possible to ascertain whether this specimen and some other more fragmentary fossils associated with it possess all of the features unique to our living species. However, the Herto fossil is certainly the best candidate yet for membership in *Homo sapiens* from this very early time. In 2005 scientists redated a skull from Omo, in Ethiopia, that is often viewed as an early *Homo sapiens*, to as long ago as 195,000 years. However, this fossil is not a completely modern *Homo sapiens* in all respects, though it, too, is close. Some very fragmentary 115,000-year-old fossils found at the mouth of South Africa's Klasies River appear close to being fully human. A partial cranium from Singa, in the Sudan, is probably more than 130,000 years old. Border Cave, on South Africa's frontier with Swaziland, has also yielded fairly modern-looking human fossils that may be over 100,000 years old, although this date has been questioned. All of these occurrences, and more, point toward an early African origin for the distinctively modern human morphology (body form). But in all of these cases either the fossils are fragmentary, their morphology cannot be exactly determined, or their dating is uncertain.

A better combination of clear morphology and reliable early dating comes from the Levant, specifically Israel, which lies in an area often

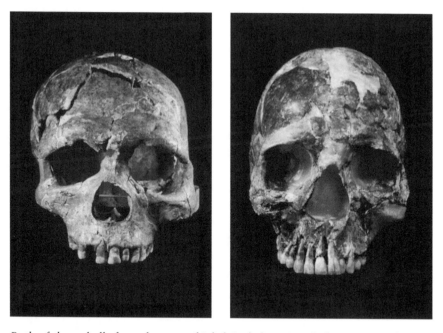

Both of these skulls from the cave of Jebel Qafzeh, in Israel, date to more than 90,000 years ago. But while the skull on the right is structured like a fully modern Homo sapiens, *with its face tucked right under the front of its tall skull, the left one has a slightly larger brain yet retains some archaic skull features, such as the heavy and continuous ridges above the eyes. Photos © Jeffrey Schwartz.*

viewed in biological terms as an extension of Africa. At the site of Jebel Qafzeh, for example, was found a burial, now dated to more than 92,000 years ago, of an individual who was very clearly an anatomically modern *Homo sapiens*. Other hominid fossils buried at the same site look rather more archaic, however, so it is not entirely clear what we ought to make of the Qafzeh hominid fossil sample as a whole. But whatever the exact facts of the matter, it is already clear that the emergence of modern human morphology—of the first individuals on Earth who looked just like us—preceded the arrival of modern behavior patterns. For the Ethiopian hominids from Herto are associated with archaic stone tools, and those from Klasies, in South Africa, possessed a Middle Stone Age technology, the equivalent of that possessed by the Neanderthals. What's more, the stone tools associated with the Qafzeh hominids were effectively indistinguishable from those made by Neanderthals in the same region.

Undoubtedly the best early evidence we have for hominids who both looked and behaved as we do comes from relatively recent times. About 40,000 years ago, the first anatomically modern *Homo sapiens* arrived in Europe. We call these hominids the Cro-Magnons, after the site in western France at which their remains were first found. Although Cro-Magnon sites have been dated to around 40,000 years in the western part of Europe (Spain) as well as in the farther reaches of eastern Europe, it is likely that these first modern immigrants arrived from the east. They might have been descendants of the early modern *Homo sapiens* found in the Levant, or they might more probably have been the descendants of a later wave of emigration from Africa. In either case, when they departed for points north and west, these early emigrants were still wielding the same Middle Paleolithic (literally, Middle Old Stone Age) technology that their forebears and the Neanderthals had used. But at some point in their journey, the ancestral Cro-Magnons invented the technology known as the Aurignacian (for the site of Aurignac, in southern France; the makers of this industry are known as Aurignacians). This new industry was wielded by the first of a succession of so-called Upper Paleolithic (Late Old Stone Age) cultures that endured in Europe until the end of the last ice age, about 10,000 years ago.

The new approach to toolmaking involved shaping a cylindrical stone core using a material such as flint that would fracture in predictable ways, then striking numerous long, thin "blades" (very different from the fat flakes of the Middle Paleolithic) successively from this core. And technological innovation did not stop there. Most important, the Aurignacians had started making implements from softer (but still du-

Powerful images of horses and a woolly rhinoceros decorate the walls of the Chauvet cave, in the Ardèche Valley of southern France. At well over 30,000 years old, they are the world's first known paintings. Photo courtesy of Jean Clottes.

rable) materials, such as bone and antler, that had rarely been exploited by Neanderthals, and then only in the crudest ways. The defining implement of the Aurignacian is, in fact, a finely shaped bone point that is split at the base, almost certainly to aid in attaching it to a spear shaft. The Aurignacians also made a variety of other useful and decorative objects from bone and antler, as well as modifying stone blades into many specialized tool types.

But the Neanderthals had made beautiful tools as well, and it is not through their production of practical utensils, even from softer materials, that we can best infer that the Cro-Magnons had a sensibility fully equivalent to our own. For in addition to the evidence of their ingenious technologies, the Cro-Magnons left behind them a wide array of proofs of their extraordinary cognitive capacities. More than 32,000 years ago they created finely drawn animal figures, liberally interspersed with obscure geometric and abstract signs, on the walls of the cave of Chauvet in southern France. In this way they inaugurated an artistic tradition that was to endure for well over 20,000 years, and that would include some of the most powerful and expressive art ever made in any period of human history.

As old as or older than the Chauvet cave art are early carvings best exemplified by objects found at early Aurignacian sites in Germany. From the cave of Vogelherd, near Ulm, has come a series of animal figurines. Of these the most impressive is a two-inch-long horse carved of mammoth ivory that was worn by someone as a pendant, perhaps 34,000 years ago. Most remarkable is that this delicate object is no literal representation of the chunky, pony-like horses that roamed the Ice Age steppes of Europe. With its graceful, flowing lines, it is an elegant evocation of the abstract essence of the horse. In the nearby cave of Hohlenstein-Stadel was found a larger piece, just as old and equally symbolic but in a different way, combining the body of a standing human with the head of a lion. In 2004 a similar image was found in another local cave, which indicates that these pieces formed part of a common local iconography. From the rock overhang of Blanchard, in France, a small, flat piece of bone of around the same age bears markings that are clearly notations, even if they might not represent a lunar calendar, as one scholar has suggested.

At Blanchard, and at various cave sites in the Pyrenees Mountains more than 30,000 years old, have been found flutes (mostly made with vulture bones) with complex sound capabilities; and if the Aurignacians thus made music, there can be no doubt that they sang and danced as well and told each other stories next to the fires that burned outside the huts they sheltered in. In the Czech Republic the archaeological site of Dolni Věstonice, nearly 30,000 years old, contained molded ceramic figurines that had been fired at high temperatures in simple but effective kilns; at the same site delicate bone needles with eyes were found that announce the advent of tailored clothing. A less elegant but still functional needle found in Slovenia dates from the very beginning of the Aurignacian, maybe 10,000 years earlier.

There is surprisingly little evidence of Aurignacian burial, but Upper Paleolithic burial soon became complex, and graves were sometimes crammed with grave goods, items that must have been considered useful to the deceased in an afterlife. At the Russian site of Sungir, for instance, an older man was interred some 28,000 years ago, dressed in an ornate tunic onto which hundreds of mammoth-tusk beads—each of which must have taken at least three hours to make—had been sewn. He also wore bangles, a necklace and a beaded cap, and decorative objects were found beside him. At the same place were found two children buried head-to-head, flanked by ramrod-straight mammoth tusks more than six feet long. These tusks, which would originally have been strongly curved, had been straightened artificially, though nobody knows exactly how.

Of course, not all Cro-Magnon burials were so elaborate, but even this fact presumably tells us something about Cro-Magnon society, in which not every individual could or would receive such sumptuous burial. In recent human societies ornamentation of the kind that accompanied the Sungir man has universally been a sign of high social status, and any society that could afford to deliberately bury such a wealth of artifacts must have been running a substantial economic surplus. Evidently Cro-Magnon society was complex and stratified as well as economically productive, with everything this implies for the way in which its members dealt with the world and with each other. We do not know exactly how Cro-Magnon societies were organized, but we can be fairly sure that, like our own, they were elaborately structured and governed by a complex web of rules and social obligations.

Along with all of this cultural innovation went a substantial increase in the complexity of hunting. Fish and bird bones begin to show up in large numbers at hominid archaeological sites for the first time in Cro-Magnon living areas; and fish and birds require more intricate hunting technology to catch than do larger animals. By the end of Cro-Magnon times, around 9,000 or 10,000 years ago, barbed harpoons, spear-throwers, and even the bow and arrow had been invented, and some authorities think that in some Cro-Magnon engravings they can discern representations of snares, used for trapping birds. Living sites became larger and more elaborate, with frequent evidence of constructed shelters and a clear division of space according to activities. A list of Cro-Magnon achievements could go on almost indefinitely, but these examples should by themselves be enough to demonstrate, beyond any doubt whatever, that the Cro-Magnons were just like us, with all of the mental equipment that we bring to bear on our own interactions with each other and the world today. By 40,000 years ago, then, modern humans were already around, with a vengeance.

But although it is the most extensive archaeological record of its kind, and is thrown into particularly dramatic relief by its contrast with the essentially symbol-free traces left by the Neanderthals in the same region, the Cro-Magnon record is far from the earliest sign we have of the arrival of the modern human sensibility. We have to look back to Africa for the first evidence of modern human behaviors, as well as for that of the distinctive modern human anatomy.

The archaeological record from the last hundred thousand years or so in Africa is less complete now than it almost certainly will eventually become, as more sites are discovered and excavated. But we are already beginning to pick up hints of the sorts of activity that we associate with modern *Homo sapiens* from remarkably early dates. The production of blade tools, for example, began in eastern Africa as much as 250,000 years ago, even though this type of tool did not become common until much later. It is not entirely clear how much we can infer about cognition from purely technological evidence of this kind, but at a similarly early time is found the first evidence for the grinding of pigments, and the long-distance exchange of useful or desirable materials seems to have started well over 100,000 years ago—although, again, it was a long time before this became a regular part of hominid life.

In contrast to the rather haphazard site structure of earlier hominids, some archaeologists believe they can detect an organized use of living space by around 100,000 years ago at such localities as the caves of Klasies River Mouth, close to Africa's southern tip. More tellingly, at Blombos Cave, a bit to the west of Klasies, have been found flat pieces of ochre some 75,000 years old and engraved with geometric designs. Many accept these as the world's earliest symbolic objects, and they are accompanied by pierced shells that may have been strung for personal adornment, another unique habit of modern *Homo sapiens*. Barbed harpoon points made of bone, and of a sophistication unmatched in Europe until around 20,000 years ago, have been found at a site in Central Africa that may be as much as 80,000 years old. Sparse as the record is, discoveries such as these strongly suggest that it was in Africa, during the period following 100,000 years ago, that the possibilities opened up by a new behavioral potential were somehow being first explored by its possessor—even though these developments were not necessarily ancestral in a linear sense to later expressions elsewhere.

There is no deeper mystery in the entire long biological history of humankind than how we came to acquire our distinctive mental qualities. It is possible to infer that for the most part—with the exception of the first upright bipeds and the first possessors of human body proportions—successful new kinds of hominid had mostly done what their predecessors had done, if a little better. But in the behavioral realm *Homo sapiens* as we know it today is a totally unprecedented kind of being. Not only do fully modern humans have a unique way of dealing with the world they inhabit, but the very pattern of behavioral innovation changed with the appearance of modern behaviors, picking up a tempo never witnessed before. Clearly, the acquisition of what has been termed "the human capacity" cannot have been a matter of fine-tuning over the eons by inexorable natural selection. Instead, this capacity was something entirely new—and not simply an extrapolation of trends that had preceded it in hominid history.

As far as we can tell from the archaeological record, the difference in cognitive capacity between *Homo sapiens* and even its closest extinct relatives is a huge one. And it is not just a difference of degree. It is a difference in kind. It is probably fair to say that even such evidently complex beings as chimpanzees do not in essence do much more than react fairly directly to stimuli that they receive from the outside world, even though those reactions may be mediated by long experience and by complex mental processing. Human beings, on the other hand, are symbolic creatures. Inside their heads they break down the outside world into a mass of mental symbols, then recombine those symbols to re-create that world. What they subsequently react to is often the mental construct, rather than the primary experiences themselves. And such re-creations differ from person to person and from society to society, which is what ultimately lies behind most of the conflicts and disagreements that we encounter in recorded human history.

Of course, we humans do exhibit reflexive and emotional responses as well as intellectual ones, and these are omnipresent reminders of our long and cumulative evolutionary past. But what marks us as so different from other living forms is this rational and objectively calculating mental layer that makes us able to ask questions such as "what if?" Yet even if this difference between us and the rest of the living world appears to be a qualitative, discontinuous one, it is nonetheless evident that human beings with the capacity for symbolic thought evolved from a precursor species without this capacity. How could this leap have been made?

This question has been with us since the first stirrings of the realization that *Homo sapiens* has a common origin with apes, primates, mammals, and ever-widening circles of other organisms. Indeed, it lay at the root of the only deep philosophical rift that ever developed in the relationship between Charles Darwin and Alfred Russel Wallace, the co-inventors of the notion of evolution by natural selection. Darwin was content to explain the acquisition of our species' cognitive abilities as a result of the pressure of natural selection on our precursors over long periods of time. And most scientists today, it would seem, concur with him. After all, to some of the most intelligent members of an intelligent species, it seems self-evident that even a tiny bit of extra intelligence is advantage enough to give its possessors a reproductive edge, generation after generation.

Wallace, however, simply could not see how natural selection could have bridged the gap between the human cognitive state and that of all other life forms. What he did see was the breadth and depth of the discontinuity between symbolic and nonsymbolic cognitive states, and he saw how the one could not be simply an extension of the other. Stymied by his inability to implicate natural selection, Wallace came to see the supernatural as the agent of the modern intellect's origin. He has been pilloried for this interpretation ever since—but in fact his basic perception was a very penetrating one.

Wallace clearly realized that natural selection is not a creative force, calling new and more desirable structures into existence at will. To the contrary: natural selection can only deal with what is there already. Biologically speaking, function has to follow form. Innovations have to arise spontaneously, and in this sense they must always arise not as *adaptations*—features that fit them to a particular way of life—but as *exaptations*—new features that are not related to current circumstances but that are potentially available to be used in new ways. The quintessential example of an exaptation is feathers, used by birds as bodily insulation for millions of years before finally being co-opted for the flight that they made possible. In the case of the evolution of human cognition we also have to realize that some features are emergent—that is, more than simply the sum of their parts. The classic example of an emergent quality is water, whose properties, so essential to life on Earth, are not predicted by those of either of its components, hydrogen and oxygen. Something totally new results from the combination of those two elements.

Almost certainly, the emergence of our cognitive capacities resulted from a similar convergence of unrelated features. By the time *Homo sapiens* appeared, the human brain must have evolved, for whatever reasons, to a point at which a small genetic change (perhaps with profound developmental consequences) was sufficient to produce a structure with an entirely new potential. For all that we know about the functions of various brain structures, we do not yet have any idea how a mass of chemical and electrical signals exchanged between neurons becomes transformed into what we experience as human consciousness. As a result, it is not at all clear what that final physical innovation might have been that made our immediate precursor at least potentially capable of symbolic thought. But it is fairly evident that we will never be able to illuminate that final leap without evoking the phenomena of exaptation and emergence. Fortunately, these processes are quite routine and do not require special explanation in themselves, however amazing their results may be.

But this cannot be the whole story. As far as we know, modern human anatomy was in place well before *Homo sapiens* began behaving in the ways that are familiar today. For example, early moderns from Jebel Qafzeh left a material record more or less indistinguishable from that left by the Neanderthals. It is highly unlikely that a symbolically reasoning hominid would have left a tangible record of this kind, or that it would have coexisted or alternated for so long with Neanderthals, as early anatomical *Homo sapiens* did in the Levant. Despite their physical modernity, it is unlikely that those inhabitants of Jebel Qafzeh behaved as humans would shortly begin to do farther south, in Africa.

What seems most likely to have happened in the sequence of events leading to the emergence of modern sensibility is thus the following. The underlying anatomical substrate for symbolic thought was born with the major structural adjustment that gave rise to our species—but was not expressed immediately in new behaviors. It must have lain fallow for many millennia, until its unprecedented uses were discovered by human ancestors who had until then possessed this new capacity unknowingly. The story seems to be that, with the necessary biological structures in place, this new potential awaited its "release," not by any biological innovation but by a cultural stimulus of some kind.

What could this cultural releaser have been? Many researchers believe that it was the development of language. And we must bear in mind that, by the time *Homo sapiens* became symbolic, it already possessed the peculiar form of the vocal tract that allows articulate speech. Clearly, this structure evolved initially in some context other than language, for there is little doubt that linguistic beings would not routinely have left behind the entirely nonsymbolic archaeological record seen at sites from Bodo to Qafzeh. The fundamental innovation that we see with the Cro-Magnons and their African precursors is that of symbolic thought, and this is something with which language is virtually synonymous. Like thought, language involves forming and manipulating symbols in the mind, and our capacity for symbolic reasoning is almost inconceivable in its absence. Imagination and creativity are part of the same process, for only once we have created mental symbols can we combine them in new ways and ask "what if?" Language is particularly attractive in this role because it is an external, communal property, in contrast to other potential releasers such as "theory of mind"—the ability to read the minds of others. Unless, that is, the primary function of language is to promote thought, rather than communication.

Intuitive, nonsymbolic reasoning can, of course, take one a long way; indeed, we can probably look upon the considerable achievements of the Neanderthals as the ultimate example of what intuition can do. But there's little doubt that it is symbolic thought that above all differentiates us from them. Indeed, that separates us not only from every other hominid but also from every other organism that has ever existed. Still, the underlying capacity that was released in this way is clearly a rather generalized ability that permits a huge variety of different behaviors that had never been possible before—a far larger number than any one individual could ever display. It is perhaps not surprising, then, that the myriad uses of this capacity were not all expressed at once. Instead, the record seems to show that the early history of modern humans was one of the sequential discovery of the things that symbolic thought made possible. This is, indeed, an ongoing process: even today we are discovering new ways in which to employ and express our unprecedented cognitive abilities.

However it came about, the origin of the human capacity for thought was a rather recent happening and an emergent one. It did not result from a gradual process of perfecting earlier trends. Much as paleoanthropologists like to think of our evolution as a linear process, a gradual progression from primitiveness to perfection, this holdover from earlier days of the science is clearly in error. We are not the result of constant fine-tuning over the eons, any more than we are the summit of creation. Of course, as a result of its long and complicated evolutionary history, *Homo sapiens* is not a purely rational animal, for our species' new and revolutionary abilities are simply new layers upon a much more ancient base. And despite our dubious track record, we should probably be grateful for this fact. For although a mechanically perfected *Homo sapiens* would lack hate, jealousy, and greed, it would presumably also be bereft of love, generosity, and hope.

So what, exactly, happened when the clearly language-bearing Cro-Magnons entered the domain of the presumptively non-language-bearing Neanderthals some 40,000 years ago? Those who wish to see *Homo neanderthalensis* as simply a variant of *Homo sapiens* would claim that the disappearance of the distinctive Neanderthal morphology within a dozen millennia of the arrival of the Cro-Magnons was due to a genetic "swamping" of the Neanderthals by the immigrants, as the sparsely scattered locals interbred with a steady stream, if not torrent, of arriving strangers. But the scale of the physical differences between the two strongly suggests otherwise. There may have been instances of what one might delicately call "Pleistocene hanky-panky" during the fairly short period when the two species shared the European subcontinent; but it is highly improbable that there was any significant, large-scale integration of the two gene pools.

Still, if the two different kinds of hominid did not interbreed and combine into a single larger entity, what did happen? There are two major possibilities, and probably both played a role in the drama. Two hominids sharing the same landscape would almost certainly have found themselves in competition. That competition might have been purely economic, with the two species physically avoiding each other but using the same resources. If this was the case, the disappearance of the Neanderthals would suggest that they were simply outcompeted by *Homo sapiens,* who exploited those resources more efficiently. It has recently been suggested that the Cro-Magnons were greater economic generalists than the Neanderthals, who specialized in hunting the megafauna; this would certainly have given the newcomers the edge. Yet at the same time it also appears likely that the two populations found themselves in physical conflict at least occasionally and in certain places.

Although (or perhaps because) it is the Cro-Magnons' creativity that we find most impressive about them, these people, like us, certainly also had a dark side. And it may well have been expressed in the Neanderthals' disappearance. The recorded history of *Homo sapiens* has not in general been one of benevolent treatment of residents by invaders, and it is likely that human nature has not changed one iota since Cro-Magnon times. But whatever the exact nature of the interaction, it is highly unlikely that the Neanderthals were forced to cede the world to *Homo sapiens* because of any *physical* disadvantage on their part. Almost certainly it was the newcomers' mental equipment, their unprecedented way of viewing and interacting with the world around them, that made the difference.

Archaeologists have discerned certain short-lived local cultures that may indicate some kind of cultural interchange between Neanderthals and Cro-Magnons. At several sites in France and Spain that date from about 36,000 to 32,000 ago (that is, from within the early phase of Cro-Magnon presence), has been found an industry known as the Châtelperronian. The Châtelperronian also has equivalents in Italy and central Europe, and all exhibit elements of both the Mousterian (Neanderthal) and the Aurignacian (Cro-Magnon) stoneworking traditions. About half of the stone implements produced by the Châtelperronians were flakes produced using the Levallois prepared-core technique used by the Neanderthals. But among Châtelperronian products are also stone tools characteristic of the Cro-Magnon tradition. And to the Châtelperronian as well are attributed objects of bone and ivory, notably (and somewhat controversially) body ornaments from the French site of Arcy-sur-Cure that include a carefully shaped pendant.

Who made the Châtelperronian artifacts? Human remains have been found with materials from this culture at only two sites, and those

Although they were probably all made by Neanderthals, about half of the tools found at Châtelperronian sites are blades, strips of stone more than twice as long as they are wide. Such tools are most commonly associated with the Cro-Magnons. Photo by Alain Roussot.

remains are those of Neanderthals. If the Châtelperronians were thus Neanderthals, how did they obtain the body ornaments? Had they learned from the invading Cro-Magnons how to work bone and ivory? Had they obtained the items from Cro-Magnons by trade? By theft? By force? Had a gifted Neanderthal stumbled over a Cro-Magnon campsite and figured out how to make the strange objects its occupants had left behind? The possibilities are endless, and it is likely that we will never know for sure, although the fact that the Châtelperronian stone tool kit included Cro-Magnon-style artifacts such as burins (boring tools) may imply that some learning by contact was involved. But whatever the exact nature of the interaction between Cro-Magnon and Neanderthal, that interaction was quite short-lived, as was the Châtelperronian period itself. At two French sites the Châtelperronian and Aurignacian alternate in the archaeological strata over a short window of time; but the cultures remain distinct, and the general pattern all over Europe is of a fairly abrupt replacement of the Mousterian by the Aurignacian.

The upshot is that, however *Homo neanderthalensis* and *Homo sapiens* interacted in Europe, the final outcome is clear: within a relatively brief time, the Neanderthals disappeared forever. And fossil datings suggest that something similar was happening at about the same time to *Homo erectus* in eastern Asia—as presumably it was to hominids in various other parts of the world, too. For example, the jury is still out on the peculiar phenomenon of *Homo floresiensis*, a short-statured and small-brained hominid described not long ago from the Indonesian island of Flores, where it appears to have survived until under 20,000 years ago. If this is indeed a dwarfed island species of hominid with its roots deep in time it, too, most likely met its end at the hands of *Homo sapiens*.

Back at the western end of the Eurasian landmass, a number of variants of the Neanderthals' "Mousterian" culture have been recognized. On the whole, however, the Neanderthals' technological production remained rather uniform over the entire huge expanse of time and space they inhabited. Not so that of the Cro-Magnons. With the arrival of *Homo sapiens* in Europe, the pace of technological change picked up dramatically. In every valley, it seems, local populations were developing their own local traditions, maybe even speaking their own dialects. Over the course of the Upper Paleolithic, the Cro-Magnons' heyday between about 40,000 and 10,000 years ago, archaeologists recognize four major cultural traditions in Europe, each marked by its own characteristic expressions and named for the particular site at which it was first identified. Each tradition lasted a longer or shorter period depending on location, but broadly they can be described as follows.

The Aurignacian, brought into Europe by the first Cro-Magnons about 40,000 years ago, expressed most of the innovations already mentioned: early cave painting, music, carving, engraving, notation, and so forth. About 28,000 years ago the Aurignacian culture disappeared and was replaced by a culture known as the Gravettian, which produced the earliest ceramic art, complex dwellings, elaborate burial, and sculpture on rock walls and is known for the "Venus" figures (female representations usually with exaggerated breasts and bellies) produced in a variety of materials. About 22,000 years ago, the Gravettian was succeeded in some places by the Solutrean, which many consider to be the high point of Stone Age flint-tool production, with its long, graceful, and exquisitely worked "laurel-leaf" points, many of which were far too delicate to have been anything but ceremonial. Some Solutrean cave art, like the Aurignacian before it, shows a command of form as fine as anything ever achieved subsequently. The final phase of the Upper Paleolithic era was the Magdalenian, which lasted from about 18,000 years ago (the coldest point of the last glacial period) to about 10,000 years ago, when the climate began warming and the enormous northern ice cap started to break up.

The Magdalenian period witnessed the greatest flowering of Ice Age art, in terms of both cave painting and "portable art" (small engravings or carvings on pieces of tusk, bone, or antler). And it also saw the development of some of the most sophisticated European hunting and gathering technology, with spear-throwers becoming common equipment and, at the very end of the period, the invention of the bow and arrow. Still, while the Magdalenian may have been the apogee of Late Ice Age cultural achievement, the Upper Paleolithic as a whole was a period of extraordinary technological exploration and ferment, despite the fact that it experienced the most extreme climatic conditions that the last ice age had to offer.

Indeed, cold times in Ice Age Europe were not necessarily hard times for crafty hunter-gatherers who were armored against the elements with clothing, tents, and other forms of culturally-generated protection. For when it was cold the principal landscape of Europe was one of open steppes and tundra, over which large-bodied grazing mammals—reindeer, cattle, horses, mammoths, woolly rhinos, and myriad others—roamed in enormous numbers, offering an endless and predictable resource upon which hominids could rely for sustenance. In warmer times the environment changed, and forests of birch, oak, fir, and beech spread over much of the land. In such conditions it was much harder for humans to make a living, for hunting deer or wild boar darting through forest glades is a much tougher and more time-consuming proposition than ambushing huge herds of reindeer out on the open steppes.

It is almost certainly as a result of such change that the high cultures of the Cro-Magnons came to an end after about 10,000 years ago. With climatic warming and the spread of forests, the numbers of open-country grazing animals dwindled and, along with them, the resource on which the Ice Age hunters had depended. And although the Cro-Magnons' accommodation to their new conditions gave rise to what were probably some of the most technically sophisticated hunting-gathering societies known in the archaeological record, material richness declined. The sophisticated representational and geometrical art of the Magdalenians was replaced by simpler painted dots on stone plaques, and the focus of cultural, economic, and technological innovation shifted to the east, where the era of settled agriculture was about to dawn.

CHAPTER 7

Settled Life

R ight through the end of the Paleolithic period (the "Old Stone Age") at about 10,000 years ago, human beings and their precursors had been more or less constantly on the move. They had lived a lifestyle of hunting and gathering that, even after they started to establish home bases, had involved picking up and moving regularly. Once *Homo sapiens* was on the scene, hominids had probably altered their activities from those of foragers, who simply roam around the landscape, opportunistically availing themselves of resources they encounter, to those of collectors, who keep a close eye on the food sources around them and plan the exploitation of local resources accordingly. But traditional practices must have continued to dictate an essentially mobile lifestyle.

Toward the end of the last Ice Age, some Upper Paleolithic peoples had already developed ways of extending their sojourns in particular places. For example, at the Ukrainian site of Mezhirich, people some 15,000 years ago built elaborate huts made from mammoth bones that clearly anticipated later village life in the sense that the huts were apparently arranged in a formal way and were probably occupied for weeks if not months at a time. Prolonged stays of this kind were made possible by the development of a storage technology that involved digging pits down into the permafrost, the constantly frozen subsurface soil. In these natural freezers, meat could be preserved for weeks or months, so that sustenance was available even when the herds of reindeer and other grazers on which the inhabitants depended had moved away to distant pastures.

It is also possible, if unproven, that at least at some times and places Upper Paleolithic hunters maintained a very close relationship with the herding animals on which they depended—perhaps somewhat in the manner of the Lapps and some Siberian peoples in recent times, who partially domesticate reindeer herds and move along with them as they migrate to fresh grazing areas. What is more, the cultures of the

Mesolithic ("Intermediate Stone Age") period, which followed the societies of the Upper Paleolithic in the new and more difficult postglacial environmental conditions, may have included some of the most highly developed hunting-and-gathering societies that ever existed. Mesolithic peoples probably quite often settled seasonally in places that were suitable for specialized occupations such as fishing. But although a tendency thus already existed toward extended periods of residence at any one spot, truly settled existence had to await the revolutionary inventions, somewhat more than 10,000 years ago, of plant cultivation and, perhaps a bit later, of the full domestication of animals.

The environmental changes resulting from climate swings at the end of the last Ice Age had a considerable impact upon the populations of *Homo sapiens* that were by then scattered widely throughout the Old World. And as might be expected, the reaction by *Homo sapiens* to those changes was totally different from the responses of earlier hominid species that had doubtless experienced similar climatic fluctuations. An area that was particularly affected by late-Pleistocene climate change was the Levant (the area bordering the eastern Mediterranean) and the lands to its north and east, particularly in the regions that are now Iraq and Turkey. This larger area is often referred to as the "Fertile Crescent," which arcs north from Israel through Syria and Turkey and down again into Iraq and Iran. In this great swath of land it appears that people who had come to depend for their sustenance on collecting wild cereals (and even earlier on the seeds of wild grasses; a dietary shift toward grains can be seen in a site in Israel as old as 23,000 years) found themselves faced at the end of the Pleistocene with longer, hotter summers and increasing aridity, which lowered the natural production of this vital resource.

To compensate for this, between about 11,000 and 10,000 years ago, the peoples of the Fertile Crescent initiated a process of cultivation and artificial selection. They planted seeds of wild cereal varieties, such as einkorn and emmer (both ancient types of wheat), that retained their seeds most effectively during harvesting and that bore those seeds in concentrated clusters. The earliest grain cultivators would also have applied another level of selection by planting the seeds of the most vigorous and productive individuals of their preferred species. At first, such planting was done to supplement the gathering of wild cereals, and only later would it have become a mainstay. The radical innovation in human economic and social existence that this development heralded may well have been spurred by climatic change, but it was made possible by the convergence of a number of unrelated factors that must have included social and technological innovations, as well as the availability in the local environment of species suitable for domestication.

Wheat was soon joined as a cultivated crop in the Fertile Crescent by barley and by legumes such as lentils and chickpeas. Just a few miles north of the better-known Neolithic site of Jericho, in the Jordan Valley, lies what remains of Netiv Hagdud, a farming village that was occupied between about 9,800 and 9,500 years ago. Excavated in the 1980s, Netiv Hagdud provides a unique glimpse of the very beginnings of farming in the Fertile Crescent. The site covers about four acres and preserves the floors and foundations of a number of square and oval mud-brick houses. It is hard to know exactly how these structures were used by their inhabitants, but it is estimated that the village housed some twenty to thirty families, a total of between 100 and 200 people. This would make Netiv Hagdud about average in size for the time, with a population about half that of Jericho but considerably larger than that of some other contemporaneous settlements.

Careful analysis of animal bones and plant parts excavated at Netiv Hagdud shows that the people who lived there collected a wide range of resources from the productive local environment—more than fifty species of nuts, fruits, and other plant parts, plus invertebrates, fish, reptiles, birds, and mammals up to the size of the mountain gazelle, a favorite prey. They extensively harvested wild grasses that were abundantly available locally; but some of the barley remains they left behind show evidence of an early stage of domestication. This suggests that the people of Netiv Hagdud, while remaining energetic hunters and gatherers, had already begun artificial cultivation as early as 9,800 years ago, possibly as a response to climatic cooling that reduced the productivity of plants in the natural environment. In any event, this site does show clearly that in a rich enough natural environment it is possible for humans to live an effectively permanent settled existence without having elaborate techniques of plant domestication—or any techniques at all of animal husbandry. Several structures at the site appear to have been used as grain storage bins. And it seems that even at this very early stage of crop growing, when cultivated grains only provided a small proportion of total food supplies, surpluses were harvested during the ripening season for consumption at other times of year.

Farther afield, rice was being cultivated in China around 7,000 years ago, and sorghum was planted in Africa earlier than that. Even in the New World, where human beings arrived relatively late, only around 15,000 to 30,000 years ago, cultivation of local plants began rather early. Evidence has recently been reported from Ecuador of squash and gourd cultivation at sites dated to between 12,000 and 10,000 years ago, and evidence of squash plantings from around 10,000 years ago has also been reported in Mexico. In Central America the early cultivation of beans and maize dates back at least as far as 7,000 years. The histories of plant domestication in different places depended on the particular species that were naturally available locally to the early cultivators. But once the principle of plant cultivation had been established, the practice expanded very rapidly, especially considering that human populations at this stage of prehistory were very sparsely distributed over the face of the world.

The earliest animal of all to be domesticated by humans was the dog (although it may well be the case that wild dogs "adopted" humans rather than the other way around). In what is now Iraq, dogs were domesticated by about 12,000 years ago, and this may already have happened a couple of thousand years earlier in northern Europe, where Mesolithic peoples quite likely used dogs when hunting forest animals. Goats, quickly followed by sheep, were being domesticated in the Fertile Crescent by around 10,000 years ago. Both animals were already abundant in the local environment and had been hunted since time immemorial. Within a thousand years of that, pigs were also being raised in this region, along with cattle, which had been domesticated in Africa around the same time. By about 5,000 to 7,000 years ago, agricultural practices of one kind or another had spread to most human-inhabited regions of the world. And at the same time the process was well under way of the worldwide peripheralization, and ultimately the exclusion, of the ancestral hunting-gathering lifestyle.

When evidence of an important invention is found in different regions of the world for about the same time, many scholars are reflexively attracted to so-called diffusionist explanations, which hold that innovations invariably spread out from a single place of origin via exploration or cultural contact. It is now becoming clear that the early development of agriculture cannot be accurately described in this way. Similar inventions have frequently been made more or less simultaneously in different places at moments when conditions were right, and archaeologists have identified seven or eight "agricultural epicenters" in which animal and plant husbandry were developed independently during the early part of what is known as the Holocene (Recent) epoch. This is the name given to our own period of geological history, the 12,000 years or so since the end of the last Ice Age—though despite this separate name there is no evidence that we are actually out of the Pleistocene cycle of alternating cold and warmer conditions.

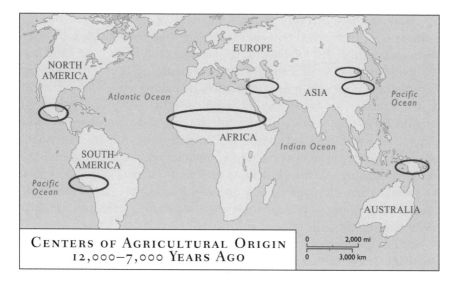

Centers of Agricultural Origin. *Scientists believe that agriculture was invented independently in these seven separate areas of the world, following the end of the ice ages, some 12,000 to 7,000 years ago.*

The centers of ancient agricultural origin, or at least of plant domestication, include the Fertile Crescent, a strip along the southern fringes of the Sahara, two river valleys in China, parts of Central and South America, and New Guinea. In each of these areas a characteristic local variety of plants and animals was domesticated: for instance, sheep, goats, and barley in the Near East; rice and water buffalo in China; llamas, maize, and beans in Central America; and bananas, sugarcane, and taro in New Guinea. What was the imperative for these innovations? Apart from responding to climatic conditions, the domestication of animals has several other advantages. Among these is that livestock is often worth more on the hoof than dead, for some animals provide resources—milk, wool, and labor, for instance—that can be collected on an ongoing basis.

As far as plants are concerned, in good years many cultivated varieties can return a fifty-fold return on seeds planted; and the consequent surpluses open up enormous new economic vistas. Human beings are endowed with considerable ingenuity; and once their new way of dealing with the world was in place, it was only a matter of time before they began to explore the radically new lifestyles and economic pursuits that their new cognitive powers made possible.

Back in the nineteenth century, an English antiquarian named Sir John Lubbock proposed that the Stone Age should be divided into two distinct periods: the "Palaeolithic," or the Old Stone Age, and the "Neolithic," the New Stone Age. The Paleolithic is the time during which stone tools were produced entirely by flaking stone with a hard or a soft hammer, or by shattering it on an anvil. From its beginnings around 2.5 million years ago, this tradition of toolmaking lasted in some places only until the end of the last ice age some 10,000 years ago, whereas in others (such as highland New Guinea), it survived into the twentieth century. Lubbock defined the Neolithic period that followed as a time when, although basic stone tool blanks may have been made by chipping or pecking, such tools were regularly finished by grinding and polishing them to smooth shapes.

In Lubbock's native England the Neolithic approach to utensil production was introduced rather late, nearly a thousand years after farmers had finally figured out, some 6,700 years ago, how to adapt agricultural practices to the conditions prevailing in temperate Europe—a generally

These polished stone axe heads from Nooan in County Clare, Ireland, are typical products of Ireland's first Neolithic farmers, made some 5,000 years ago. Such implements are thought to have been used for chopping wood, and their introduction into Ireland heralded widespread deforestation. Courtesy of the National Museum of Ireland.

less propitious environment for farming than the sunnier, warmer south. But farther east and south the first signs of the Neolithic toolmaking styles go back substantially farther in time, to the end of the last ice age, when farming and settled life were becoming established in the Fertile Crescent. Indeed, it is now generally recognized that Lubbock's stone-tool-based definition of the Neolithic is more useful when expanded well beyond the production of polished stone tools, to embrace the larger lifestyle revolution ushered in by the invention of agriculture.

The Neolithic, then, began at different times in different places. And it was characterized locally by different combinations of technological, economic, and social innovations, in a pattern that was dictated by variations among local environments as well as by historical circumstances. In the Old World, for example, the Neolithic introduction of textile weaving seems to have come after the invention of pottery, whereas the reverse appears to have been the case in South America. Some Neolithic innovations were in fact revivals or rediscoveries of earlier technologies. In the Near East, for example, early Neolithic developments included multiple introductions of kiln-fired pottery objects, such as containers or bowls. Ceramic technology had already been used, but only for symbolic objects, nearly 20,000 years before at Dolní Věstonice, the Czech site where finely made needles were also found. Right at the beginning of the Neolithic, pestles and grinding slabs show up, no longer used for pulverizing pigments but for grinding the seeds of barley and emmer wheat. Textiles appeared very early in South America and were developed there independently of the making of nets about 26,000 years ago that has been documented in the Czech Republic. The Czech nets may have been used for hunting; but most of the new technologies of the Neolithic involved utensils related to a sedentary and agricultural way of life.

Profound as was the revolution of the Neolithic, however, in some places it was a relatively short stage in human history. Before Lubbock published his book *Prehistoric Times* in 1865, archaeologists had already defined a sequence in Europe of technological phases, from Stone Age to Bronze Age to Iron Age, based on the introduction of new materials into the cultural arsenal. The Neolithic arrived in Britain only about 6,000 years ago, several millennia after its appearance in the Near East; but by some 4,200 years ago it was already being superseded by Bronze Age technology. The highly episodic, even monotonous, pattern of change that had characterized the technological scene throughout almost the entire Paleolithic period had been well and truly dispelled.

The adoption of a settled existence based on agriculture resulted directly in a major shift in the structures of human societies and the types of technologies they used, although the exact responses to the new situation varied from one region to another. The change in lifestyle from mobile to settled is best documented in the area of the Fertile Crescent, where this change also seems to have happened earliest. Several archaeological sites in the Levant dating to between about 12,000 and 10,000 years ago have been attributed to a culture known as the Natufian. The Natufian people were probably only semisedentary in most places, but some of their sites are quite large and include the remains of substantial structures whose limestone foundations give them a feeling of permanence. These people also had an extensive stone toolkit that included small microliths (literally, "tiny stones") that were clearly meant to be attached to handles to form complex tools, some of which were used for harvesting grains.

Other Natufian implements included mortars and pestles that were used either for pounding nuts or for grinding or cracking grains, and bone tools such as harpoons, fishing hooks, needles, and awls. Impressions in lumps of clay found at similar sites in the region also strongly suggest that woven mats and baskets were also being used. This wide range of technologies would indicate that the Natufians already lived on quite a broad and flexible array of resources; but an economy of this kind is a very plausible precursor to a more specialized agricultural lifestyle, and almost certainly it was. Indeed, it seems that a Natufian-style tendency to stay in the same place for extended periods, based on intensive exploitation of natural resources in a particular local area, may in fact have been a prerequisite for adopting a fully settled way of life.

During the period between about 10,500 and 8,500 years ago we find in the Fertile Crescent a number of sites representing the "Pre-Pottery Neolithic." This was the period during which various animals and plants were domesticated in the region. The earliest evidence of both animal and plant domestication in the same place comes from sites such as Ganj Dareh in Iraq, a small settlement at which goats were raised and cereals were cultivated about 9,000 years ago, and Abu Hureyra, in Syria. This latter site is particularly interesting because it furnishes a continuous record of occupation throughout the period of transition: from hunting and gathering between 11,500 and 11,000 years ago, to hunting and gathering supplemented by cereal cultivation at about 10,400 years ago, and finally to both plant and animal domestication—still supplemented by hunting and gathering—by about 9,000 years ago.

Throughout nearly all of this period simple dwellings were constructed from timber and reeds, but soon afterward (including at Abu Hureyra) we begin to find substantial villages with multi-roomed mud-

Like many early settlement sites in the Near East, the successive occupation layers at Abu Hureya, in northern Syria, built up to form a tell, a high mound visible from far away. The site is now under water, having been flooded in 1974 by damming of the Euphrates. Photo by Gordon C. Hillman.

brick houses equipped with such specialized amenities as ovens and hearths. Occasionally, these spaces contained decorated walls and large sculptures, such as the ones some 8,500 years old found at Çatal Hüyük in Turkey. Numerous males buried at this site show fractured left forearms (where right-handed individuals would have held shields), and this suggests a certain amount of organized violence among communities. Recurrent violence is also implied by the apparently defensive structure of the buildings themselves, which were grouped together with a common external wall and were accessible only by retractable ladders. The necessity of defensive structures even at this early date is also hinted at in Jericho, in the Jordan Valley, where by 8,500 years ago humans were settled permanently enough that they built substantial walls apparently for protection—though these walls may also have had a role in flood control.

A typical village of the period was Çayönü, in the Turkish northern reaches of the Fertile Crescent. This settlement of 25 to 50 houses and maybe 100 to 200 inhabitants was occupied between 9,300 and 8,500 years ago, a period that straddled the domestication of sheep and goats at the site. Between 9,300 and 8,700 years ago the inhabitants lived in quite spacious houses that were arranged as in a planned community,

Archaeologists exposed human burials beneath the plaster floor of a house at Çatal Hüyük in Turkey. The people of Çatal Hüyük may have buried their ancestors below their own homes as a symbol of family ownership. Courtesy of Çatalhöyük Research Project.

and some of which were subdivided into areas for storage and living. These people cultivated emmer and einkorn wheats, and apparently hunted wild game in the surrounding region. It was late in the history of the village that domesticated sheep and goats were added to the local economy, with pigs following shortly thereafter. However, under the prevailing conditions—which presumably included a rather sparse human population—it had clearly been possible to maintain a reasonable level of affluence without the domesticated animals. This is why many believe that, in this region at least, settled life and plant domestication may have been prerequisites for animal domestication later on.

None of this means, however, that animal husbandry played a minor role in the economic development of the Fertile Crescent and the parts of the world to which its influence spread. By about 9,000 years ago the addition of goat-raising, and then sheep- and pig-raising, to cereal cultivation had laid the groundwork for a substantial economic expansion and intensification that was to have enormous consequences, especially once the plow, irrigation, and cattle raising had been added to the mix.

For these innovations were what made urbanization possible and, in doing so, set the stage for the great early civilizations.

The archaeological record shows that agriculturally based settled ways of life had begun to expand away from the Fertile Crescent and into Europe by around 7,800 years ago. These new lifestyles spread by way of the southern European coastline and, initially at least, probably depended on trading contacts, which were apparently already well established by the time domestication came in. However, the spread north as well as west of this new way of living had to await the solution of a whole suite of technical problems created by a harsher climate. Agricultural lifestyles thus did not penetrate throughout northern Europe until around 6,000 years ago.

On the Asian front, pottery showed up early in Japan at more than 12,000 years ago—but was not accompanied by cereal cultivation of any kind until about 9,000 years ago. In China, elaborate settlements with defensive walls date back to about 7,000 years ago, approximately the same time as the first rice cultivation there. Northern Africa has yielded evidence of somewhat Natufian-like hunting/fishing societies from as early as 11,000 years ago, and a distinctive kind of pottery is found there at sites that are around 8,000 years old. There is also some evidence that the domestication of certain animal and plant species in northern Africa had begun by around that time, but very early signs of permanent settlement are lacking. As for the New World, the so-called Formative stage, which saw the widespread introduction of settlement and subsistence agriculture, generally dates from rather late—around 4,000 years ago—although there is evidence of plant domestication a good deal earlier at some sites in Central America.

Hunting-gathering and other mobile lifestyles impose limits on both population size and the complexity of the economic and social organization that any particular human society can have. So although interactions among individual humans have always presumably been as intricate and murky as they are today, in pre-settled times entire societies would not have been "complex" in the strictest sense in which anthropologists use the word—even where status differences existed among individuals. This would also have been the case in the transitional phases between early settled societies and early urban ones. For by the term "complex society" archaeologists generally mean societies that are divided into distinct levels, and in which not all individuals have the same access to wealth or power. In societies with inequalities of this kind, access to economic resources and political authority is more frequently inherited than acquired, power tends to be more or less centralized, and individuals have specialized occupations.

Today, thanks to settlement and urbanization, virtually everyone lives in a complex society; yet this was not always so. It has been pointed out that a typical person living about 8,000 years ago in a village in Mesopotamia, the eastern arc of the Fertile Crescent, would have been a member of a community of a few hundred people at most, nearly all of them fairly close relatives. Almost all members of that community would have lived similar lives that revolved around daily work in the fields and would have possessed similar skills. Important life decisions would have been made within each family group. But a mere three millennia later, the record shows that life in the very same place was extraordinarily different. By 5,000 years ago, there had been a total change in the nature of Mesopotamian society—at that point, some of its members were royalty, others were craftspeople, yet others slaves. Basic life decisions affecting individuals were passed down the hierarchy, from on high, and an apparatus to enforce conformity with social norms was in place. Economic roles had become specialized: each individual plied a particular trade and was dependent on other members of the society with different skills. The town itself might have swelled to a population of thousands. For the individual in ancient Mesopotamia, the change in lifestyle that came with rapid adoption of complex social structures was enormous.

This was equally true of other parts of the world, as societies changed and evolved along with their economic bases. Archaeologists have identified five regions in addition to Mesopotamia in which autonomous complex societies spontaneously emerged in the eventful two millennia that spanned about 6,000 to 4,000 years ago. Plausibly, every other complex society today has ultimately inherited its structure from one or more of these original six, through conquest or through contact of some other kind. In the Near Eastern region, ancient Egyptian society acquired its complex structure in the period after about 5,500 years ago. In India's Indus Valley, the Harappan culture evolved out of a tradition of village farming that began to develop about 7,000 years ago and had begun the advance to a full-blown civilization by a little under 5,000 years ago. In northern and central China, early farming communities began to coalesce into complex urban societies at about the same time. It was a little later, beginning at about 3,500 years ago, that complex societies began to be seen in Central America, with the emergence of the Olmec culture. And in South America the origins of the great civilizations of the Andes can be detected earlier than that, maybe as long ago as 5,000 years.

Why this apparently inexorable worldwide tendency toward complexity? It probably has a lot to do with the inherently complex human psyche, combined with the fact that by around 6,000 to 4,000 years ago human economic structures had progressed to a point where social complexity was possible because populations of a critical minimum size could at last be maintained. A huge amount of effort has been put into specific attempts to explain why simple societies gravitate toward the complex. Earlier explanations generally tried to invoke a single overriding cause, such as simple population growth, competition with neighboring societies, the need for mechanisms to distribute the products of agriculture, the necessity of planning in larger societies, and so forth. Explanations encompassing multiple causes have since become more popular, as archaeologists now recognize that any hypothesis for the origins of social complexity has to take into account the possible ways in which a culture can change, together with external environmental pressures (which may both influence and limit the ways in which a particular society can change), and the actual mechanism of change that seems to have operated in any one case. Of course, any credible explanation necessarily has to take into consideration the unique circumstances of each particular society examined and to this extent will be less valid as a generalization about the overall process. So in the end it seems unlikely that in studying this question we will ever be able completely to avoid the murky subject of the human psyche—which is the only element common to all societies as they move from simple to complex.

The period between about 10,000 and 6,000 years ago has generally been thought of as a period of worldwide transition from purportedly simple hunting-gathering cultures to the more rooted forms we think of as "civilization." And although in one sense this perspective is undoubtedly correct, it is also somewhat misleading. This is partly because "civilization" is such a loaded and poorly defined term, applied by some scholars even to the societies of the European Upper Paleolithic. And it is partly because it implies a transition from the simple to the complex, which is really only an accurate perception in the economic and technological realms. Hunter-gatherers have a totally different perspective on the world from that of agriculturalists, it is true; but it is not necessarily a simpler one. The world views and social interactions of hunter-gatherers are (or, sadly, were) typically highly complex and nuanced, as are their interactions with the environment around them. It is even possible to argue that in abandoning ancestral ways of life for the new ones made possible—or even obligatory—by the domestication of animals and plants, humankind made a highly questionable tradeoff.

At the very least, something of value was lost, as well as gained, in this transition.

Archaeological sites such as Jericho and Çatal Hüyük certainly mark major milestones between ancestral lifestyles and later ones in the area of the Fertile Crescent. And just as certainly they provided the essential foundations on which the early Near Eastern civilizations such as those of Uruk, Sumer, and Akkad were later built. Moreover, the kind of society they represented did not last very long, at least in that region, for as populations increased it gave way with amazing rapidity to larger and more highly structured polities. Still, the expressions we see at these sites most emphatically do not mark any change in the essential nature of human beings themselves. Whether hunter-gatherers or agriculturalists, fully modern human beings have always processed their perceptions of and responses to their environment through cultural filters. These filters have ensured that the movement toward economic and social complexity in different parts of the world, even neighboring ones, has proceeded at varying rates and along different paths.

It will always be debatable whether the shift to an agricultural way of life and eventually to complex urbanized societies was a good thing, either for the planet on which we live or even for *Homo sapiens* itself. But there is no doubt that it had a revolutionary effect on the way in which we humans view ourselves and our place in the world. Anthropologists have had only a small window of opportunity to study non-agricultural societies in the century or so since their science was born. But it does appear that, in hunting-gathering communities, people tend to identify particularly closely with the environment around them, to understand that they are part of that environment, and to recognize explicitly that, because the environment feeds and clothes them, they in turn have a responsibility toward it. What is more, hunting-gathering peoples are limited by their lifestyle to living in low population densities, and their technologies are relatively simple. This inherently restricts the damage they are able to do to the world around them, even though it seems quite likely that advanced hunter-gatherer groups in the late Ice Age may have been responsible for the extinction of large-bodied animals in various parts of the world. In Australia especially, there is evidence for large-scale environmental modification through the use of fire.

The development of agriculture changed the entire calculation. Instead of living within and as part of the environment, early agricultural people found themselves in opposition to the forces of nature. Rain doesn't necessarily fall, nor does the sun shine, at the convenience of farmers. Farming productivity may vary wildly from one year to the next, precipitating economic and social crises. And when people beset by climatic vagaries begin to feel at odds with nature, they begin to lose their sense of integration with it. Life becomes a struggle to overcome nature: to modify it and, if at all possible, to dominate it. It is no coincidence that the founding documents of the Judeo-Christian religions, ultimately derived from the early farmers of the Fertile Crescent, contain what Niles Eldredge of the American Museum of Natural History has called "the most ringing declaration of independence ever set down." This is the passage from the first book of the Bible, Genesis (1: 27), which translates as "God said . . . be fruitful, and multiply, and replenish the earth, and subdue it; and have dominion . . . over every living thing that moveth upon the earth." The independence declared here is independence of our species from nature itself, based on a profound feeling of separateness from the environment on which we depend.

In its exhortation to "multiply," this passage from Genesis also encapsulates the other principal consequence of the adoption of settled lifestyles: population growth. Hunter-gatherers are inherently restricted in group size, not only by the limitations of available resources but also by the difficulties of transporting children who remain totally helpless for far longer than other mammal infants. For example, San women in the Kalahari Desert of southern Africa breastfed their infants for as much as four years. This had the effect of inhibiting their fertility for an extended period and thus reduced the number of young children they would have to handle while on the move. Behavioral expressions such as this reflect the fact that for hunter-gatherers it is more often advantageous to limit their population than to increase it.

The calculation is quite different for farmers, who always need labor to till the fields and whose fixed location makes large families practical. But the resulting population expansion has its own drawbacks. Big populations have to be fed, and even with irrigation, seed selection, and all the other tricks in the cultivator's arsenal, agricultural productivity in any given environment can fluctuate considerably over short spans of time. Grain storage and the drying of meat can help cushion the impact of poor harvests from one year to the next, but just a few years of floods or drought can wreak havoc with a delicate system. The larger the population the more vulnerable it is to environmental disruption, and even technological improvements cannot indefinitely insulate societies from the consequences of overexpansion. Indeed, technological improvements have often placed societies on a sort of economic treadmill. Time and again the archaeological record, from places all over the world, shows a similar pattern among settled societies: increasing population leads to overintensification of agricultural practices, which in turn results in economic crash and social disintegration.

We like to think that history is created by people, and we are certainly most often taught it that way; but things are not that simple. Irresistible socioeconomic forces often result from environmental pressures that are totally beyond the control of the societies concerned and of their leaders. Thus, factors that are external to individual people, or even to societies and nations themselves, have ultimately been behind a large proportion of the blossomings, breakdowns, and conflicts that make up the complex tapestry of human history.

Chronology

All dates given here are approximate and subject to varying margins of error.

6.5–4.4 MILLION YEARS AGO
Earliest hominids live in what are now the African countries of Chad (*Sahelanthropus*), Ethiopia (*Ardipithecus*), and Kenya (*Orrorin*)

4.2 MILLION YEARS AGO
Earliest definitely bipedal hominid species (*Australopithecus anamensis*) lives in Kenya

3.8–3.0 MILLION YEARS AGO
Australopithecus afarensis, the species of the 3.18-million-year-old skeleton "Lucy," lives in Ethiopia and Tanzania

2.5 MILLION YEARS AGO
First "robust" australopiths (*Paranthropus*) live in Kenya and Ethiopia; first crude stone tools are made at sites in Kenya and Ethiopia (those in Ethiopia possibly by *Australopithecus garhi*)

1.9–1.8 MILLION YEARS AGO
Homo habilis lives in Tanzania, makes simple Oldowan stone tools; *Homo ergaster* lives in Kenya

1.8–1.7 MILLION YEARS AGO
Earliest hominids live outside Africa, at Dmanisi in the Republic of Georgia; other hominids possibly reach southeast Asia

1.6 MILLION YEARS AGO
The "Turkana Boy" lives and dies in Kenya

1.5 MILLION YEARS AGO
Acheulean handaxes are invented; earliest possible use of fire by hominids at Swartkrans, South Africa, and Chesowanja, Kenya

1.4 MILLION YEARS AGO
Last robust australopiths appear in Ethiopia

800,000 YEARS AGO
Hominids live, and possibly practice cannibalism, at the Gran Dolina, in the Atapuerca Hills of Spain

800,000–700,000 YEARS AGO
Earliest definitively known campfires are used in Israel

600,000 YEARS AGO
Homo heidelbergensis appears at Bodo, Ethiopia

500,000 YEARS AGO
Homo heidelbergensis appears in Europe; hominids possibly start hunting large mammals

400,000 YEARS AGO
Homo erectus ("Peking Man") lives at Zhoukoudian, China; domestication of fire becomes widespread; soon thereafter, first known artificial shelters are built at Terra Amata, France; first known suggested throwing spears are made at Schoeningen, Germany; numerous hominids—Neanderthal relatives—are found in the Pit of the Bones at Atapuerca, Spain

300,000 YEARS AGO
Prepared-core tools begin to appear

250,000 YEARS AGO
First blade tools are made in Africa

200,000 YEARS AGO
Homo neanderthalensis appears in Europe

160,000 YEARS AGO
First possible anatomically modern *Homo sapiens* lives in Ethiopia

90,000 YEARS AGO
Anatomically modern *Homo sapiens* appears outside Africa for the first time

75,000 YEARS AGO
First symbolic objects (geometrically incised ochre tablets) are created in South Africa; for the first time, shells are pierced for stringing, in South Africa and Ethiopia

60,000 YEARS AGO
Humans occupy Australia for the first time

50,000+ YEARS AGO
Neanderthals practice deliberate burial of their dead

40,000 YEARS AGO
Homo sapiens first arrives in Europe, and possibly on Java

34,000 YEARS AGO
Earliest known cave painting, musical instruments, figurines, and notations are created in Europe

28,000 YEARS AGO
Cro-Magnons begin to practice elaborate burial with grave goods and body ornamentation

27,000 YEARS AGO
Neanderthals become extinct; earliest known nets, ceramic figurines, and slender bone needles with eyes are crafted in Europe

23,000 YEARS AGO
Humans in Israel begin to gather wild grains for food

12,000–15,000 YEARS AGO (POSSIBLY EARLIER)
First humans arrive in the Americas

12,500 YEARS AGO
First pottery is made in Japan

12,000 YEARS AGO
Dogs are domesticated in the Near East

12,000–10,000 YEARS AGO
Semisettled life begins in the Levant

10,400 YEARS AGO
Permanent settlements and grain cultivation begin in the Fertile Crescent

9,000 YEARS AGO
Goats and sheep are domesticated in the Near East

9,000–8,000 YEARS AGO
Cattle are domesticated in several regions

8,500 YEARS AGO
Fortified settlements begin to be constructed in the Near East

7,000 YEARS AGO
Rice cultivation begins in China

6,700 YEARS AGO
Farming begins in western Europe

6,000–5,000 YEARS AGO
Crop cultivation and domestication of llamas and alpacas begin in South America; complex stratified societies emerge in the Fertile Crescent and in the Indus Valley of India; Andean complex societies begin to flower at the end of this period

Further Reading

GENERAL

Conroy, Glenn C. *Reconstructing Human Origins: A Modern Synthesis*. New York: W. W. Norton, 1997.

Delson, Eric, Ian Tattersall, John Van Couvering, and Alison Brooks, eds. *Encyclopedia of Human Evolution and Prehistory*. 2nd ed. New York: Garland, 2000.

DeSalle, Rob, and Ian Tattersall. *Human Origins: From Bones to Genomes*. College Station: Texas A&M Press, 2007.

deWaal, Frans. *Our Inner Ape: A Leading Primatologist Explains Why We Are Who We Are*. New York: Riverhead, 2005.

Johanson, Donald, and Blake Edgar. *From Lucy to Language*. 2nd ed. New York: Simon & Schuster, 2006.

Jolly, Alison. *Lucy's Legacy: Sex and Intelligence in Human Evolution*. Cambridge, Mass.: Harvard University Press, 1999.

Klein, Richard. *The Human Career*. 2nd ed. Chicago: University of Chicago Press, 1999.

Stringer, Chris, and Peter Andrews. *The Complete World of Human Evolution*. London: Thames & Hudson, 2005.

Tattersall, Ian. *The Fossil Trail: How We Know What We Think We Know About Human Evolution*. New York: Oxford University Press, 1995.

Tattersall, Ian, and Jeffrey H. Schwartz. *Extinct Humans*. Boulder, Colo.: Westview, 2000.

Wood, Bernard. *Human Evolution: A Very Short Introduction*. New York: Oxford University Press, 2005.

Zimmer, Carl. *Smithsonian Intimate Guide to Human Origins*. New York: HarperCollins, 2005.

CHAPTER 1: EVOLUTIONARY PROCESSES

Carroll, Sean B. *The Making of the Fittest: DNA and the Ultimate Forensic Record of Evolution*. New York: W. W. Norton, 2006.

Coyne, Jerry A., and H. Allen Orr. *Speciation*. Sunderland, Mass.: Sinauer Associates, 2004.

Cracraft, Joel, and Rodger W. Bybee, eds. *Evolutionary Science and Society: Educating a New Generation*. Washington, D.C.: American Institute of Biological Sciences, 2007.

Cracraft, Joel, and Michael J. Donoghue, eds. *Assembling the Tree of Life*. New York: Oxford University Press, 2004.

Eldredge, Niles. *Darwin: Discovering the Tree of Life*. New York: W. W. Norton, 2005.

Gould, Stephen Jay. *The Structure of Evolutionary Theory*. Cambridge, Mass.: Belknap Press, 2002.

Pagel, Mark, ed. *Encyclopedia of Evolution*. New York: Oxford University Press, 2002.

Rice, Stanley A. *Encyclopedia of Evolution*. New York: Checkmark, 2007.

Schwartz, Jeffrey H. *Sudden Origins: Fossils, Genes, and the Origin of Species*. New York: Wiley, 1999.

Tattersall, Ian. *The Human Odyssey: Four Million Years of Human Evolution*. New York: Prentice-Hall, 1993.

———. *The Monkey in the Mirror: Essays on the Science of What Makes Us Human*. New York: Harcourt, 2002.

CHAPTER 2: FOSSILS AND ANCIENT ARTIFACTS

Arthur, Wallace. *Creatures of Accident: The Rise of the Animal Kingdom*. New York: Hill & Wang, 2006.

Gee, Henry. *In Search of Deep Time*. Ithaca, N.Y.: Cornell University Press, 1999.

Gosden, Chris. *Prehistory: A Very Short Introduction*. New York: Oxford University Press, 2003.

Marks, Jonathan. *What It Means to Be 98% Chimpanzee: Apes, People and Their Genes*. Berkeley: University of California Press, 2002.

Schwartz, Jeffrey H. *Skeleton Keys: An Introduction to Human Skeletal Morphology, Development and Analysis*. New York: Oxford University Press, 1995.

Tattersall, Ian. *The Human Odyssey: Four Million Years of Human Evolution*. New York: Prentice-Hall, 1993.

Tattersall, Ian, and Niles Eldredge. "Fact, Theory, and Fantasy in Human Paleontology." *American Scientist* 65 (1977): 204–211.

Thomson, Keith. *Fossils: A Very Short Introduction*. New York: Oxford University Press, 2005.

Van Andel, Tjeerd H. *New Views on an Old Planet*. 2nd ed. New York: Cambridge University Press, 1994.

CHAPTER 3: ON THEIR OWN TWO FEET

Bromage, Timothy G., and Friedemann Schrenk, eds. *African Biogeography, Climate Change and Human Evolution*. New York: Oxford University Press, 1999.

Gibbons, Ann. *The First Human: The Race to Discover Our Earliest Ancestors*. New York: Doubleday, 2006.

Hart, Donna, and Robert W. Sussman. *Man the Hunted: Primates, Predators and Human Evolution*. New York: Westview, 2005.

Johanson, Donald, and Maitland Edey. *Lucy: The Beginnings of Humankind*. New York: Simon & Schuster, 1981.

Kalb, Jon. *Adventures in the Bone Trade: The Race to Discover Human Ancestors in Ethiopia's Afar Depression*. New York: Copernicus Books, 2001.

Kingdon, Jonathan. *Lowly Origin: Where, When and Why Our Ancestors First Stood Up*. Princeton, N.J.: Princeton University Press, 2003.

Schwartz, Jeffrey H. *The Red Ape: Orangutans and Human Origins*. 2nd ed. New York: Westview, 2005.

Stanford, Craig B. *Upright: The Evolutionary Key to Becoming Human*. Boston: Houghton Mifflin, 2003.

Stanford, Craig B., and Henry Bunn, eds. *Meat Eating and Human Evolution*. New York: Oxford University Press, 2001.

CHAPTER 4: EMERGENCE OF THE GENUS *HOMO*

Jablonski, Nina G. *Skin: A Natural History*. Berkeley: University of California Press, 2006.

Johanson, Donald, and James Shreeve. *Lucy's Child: The Discovery of a Human Ancestor*. New York: William Morrow, 1989.

Potts, Rick. *Humanity's Descent: The Consequences of Ecological Instability*. New York: William Morrow, 1996.

Schick, Kathy D., and Nicholas Toth. *Making Silent Stones Speak: Human Evolution and the Dawn of Technology*. New York: Simon & Schuster, 1993.

Shipman, Pat. *The Man Who Found the Missing Link: Eugene Dubois and His Lifelong Quest to Prove Darwin Right*. New York: Simon & Schuster, 2001.

Swisher, Carl C. III, Garniss H. Curtis, and Roger Lewin. *Java Man: How Two Geologists' Dramatic Discoveries Changed Our Understanding of the Evolutionary Path to Modern Humans*. New York: Scribner, 2000.

van Oosterzee, Penny. *Dragon Bones: The Story of Peking Man*. Cambridge, Mass.: Perseus, 2000.

Walker, Alan, and Richard Leakey, eds. *The Nariokotome* Homo erectus *Skeleton*. Cambridge, Mass.: Harvard University Press, 1993.

Walker, Alan, and Pat Shipman. *The Wisdom of the Bones: In Search of Human Origins*. New York: Knopf, 1996.

CHAPTER 5: GETTING BRAINIER

Arsuaga, Juan Luis. *The Neanderthal's Necklace: In Search of the First Thinkers*. New York: Four Walls Eight Windows, 2002.

Finlayson, Clive. *Neanderthals and Modern Humans: An Ecological and Evolutionary Perspective*. New York: Cambridge University Press, 2004.

Mellars, Paul. *The Neanderthal Legacy: An Archaeological Perspective from Western Europe*. Princeton, N.J.: Princeton University Press, 1996.

Mithen, Steven. *The Singing Neanderthals: The Origins of Language, Mind, and Body*. Cambridge, Mass.: Harvard University Press, 2006.

Shreeve, James. *The Neandertal Enigma: Solving the Problem of Modern Human Origins*. New York: William Morrow, 1995.

Stanley, Steven M. *Children of the Ice Age: How a Global Catastrophe Allowed Humans to Evolve*. New York: Harmony, 1996.

Stringer, Chris, and Clive Gamble. *In Search of the Neanderthals: Solving the Puzzle of Human Origins*. New York: Thames & Hudson, 1993.

Tattersall, Ian. *The Last Neanderthal: The Rise, Success, and Mysterious Extinction of Our Closest Human Relatives*. Rev. ed. Boulder, Colo.: Westview Press, 1998.

van Andel, Tjeerd, and William Davies. *Neanderthals and Modern Humans in the European Landscape During the Last Glaciation*. Cambridge, U.K.: McDonald Institute, 2003.

CHAPTER 6: MODERN HUMAN ORIGINS

DeSalle, Rob, and Ian Tattersall. *Human Origins: From Bones to Genomes*. College Station: Texas A&M Press, 2007.

Klein, Richard, and Blake Edgar. *The Dawn of Human Culture*. New York: Wiley, 2002.

Koppel, Tom. *Lost World: Rewriting Prehistory—How New Science Is Tracing America's Ice Age Mariners*. New York: Atria, 2003.

Lewin, Roger. *The Origin of Modern Humans*. New York: Scientific American Library, 1993.

Olson, Steve. *Mapping Human History: Discovering the Past Through Our Genes*. Boston: Houghton Mifflin, 2002.

Relethford, John. *Reflections of Our Past: How Human History Is Revealed in Our Genes*. Cambridge, Mass.: Perseus, 2003.

Stringer, Chris, and Robin McKie. *African Exodus: The Origins of Modern Humanity*. New York: Henry Holt, 1996.

Tattersall, Ian. *Becoming Human: Evolution and Human Uniqueness*. New York: Harcourt Brace, 1998.

Wade, Nicholas. *Before the Dawn: Recovering the Lost History of Our Ancestors*. New York: Penguin, 2006.

Wells, Spencer. *The Journey of Man: A Genetic Odyssey*. Princeton, N.J.: Princeton University Press, 2002.

CHAPTER 7: SETTLED LIFE

Ammerman, Albert J., and Paolo Biagi, eds. *The Widening Harvest: The Neolithic Transition in Europe—Looking Back, Looking Forward*. Boston: Archaeological Institute of America, 2003.

Balter, Michael. *The Goddess and the Bull: Çatalhöyük: An Archaeological Journey to the Dawn of Civilization*. New York: Free Press, 2005.

Cowan, C. Wesley, and Patty Jo Watson, eds. *The Origins of Agriculture: An International Perspective*. Washington, D.C.: Smithsonian Institution Press, 1992.

Mithen, Steven. *The Prehistory of the Mind: A Search for the Origins of Art, Science and Religion*. London: Thames & Hudson, 1998.

———. *After the Ice: A Global Human History, 20,000–5,000* BC. London: Weidenfeld and Nicholson, 2003.

Price, T. Douglas, ed. *Europe's First Farmers*. New York: Cambridge University Press, 2000.

Smith, Bruce D. *The Emergence of Agriculture*. New York: Scientific American Library, 1995.

Wenke, Robert J. *Patterns in Prehistory: Mankind's First Three Million Years*. 4th ed. New York: Oxford University Press, 1999.

Websites

ANATOMY

Comparative Mammalian Brain Collections
www.brainmuseum.org
   Images and information from one of the
   world's largest collections of well-preserved, sectioned, and stained brains of
   mammals at the University of Wisconsin
   and Michigan State University Comparative
   Mammalian Brain Collections. Includes
   photographs of brains of more than 100
   species of mammals (including humans)
   representing over 20 mammalian orders.

The eSkeletons Project
www.eskeletons.org
   Digitized versions of human and non-
   human primate skeletons in two and three
   dimensions in full color and animations,
   along with supplemental information. The
   user can navigate through the various
   regions of the skeleton and view all orien-
   tations of each element along with muscle
   and joint information.

BIOLOGY/
PALEOANTHROPOLOGY

Becoming Human
www.becominghuman.org
   Run by the Institute of Human Origins, this
   site has up-to-date news stories, extinct
   hominid profiles, and an extensive glossary.

The Human Origins Program (Smithsonian Institution)
www.mnh.si.edu/anthro/humanorigins/
   Covers a range of topics including primate
   origins, human evolution, diversity and
   dispersal, as well as cultural evolution. It
   provides information and good quality
   color images of a number of extinct hominids as well as non-human primates.

Institute of Human Origins
www.asu.edu/clas/iho/
   Official website of the Institute of Human
   Origins. Contains information on the
   "Lucy" skeleton as well as news stories.

The Leakey Foundation
www.leakeyfoundation.org
   The website of a leading foundation supporting research in human evolution and
   primatology. Scientific news stories and in-
   depth features.

National Geographic Outpost: In Search of Human Origins
www.nationalgeographic.com/outpost/
   The National Geographic Society supports
   fieldwork in paleoanthropology and posts
   stories about its research on this page. The
   Interpretation Station has information
   about interpreting fossil evidence.

The Neanderthal Tools Project
www.the-neanderthal-tools.org/?page_id=7
   Currently under construction, this is an
   online database of Neanderthal finds in
   Europe. It will ultimately provide three-
   dimensional images, geo-mapping, and
   other resources.

FOSSIL AND ARCHAEOLOGICAL SITES

Atapuerca: A World Heritage Site
www.ucm.es/info/paleo/ata/english/main.htm
   Official Atapuerca site webpage. Includes
   history of the site, current research, fauna,
   tools, ecology and geology, a virtual tour of
   the fossils, a photo album, and videos of the
   site.

Boxgrove Home Page
matt.pope.users.btopenworld.com/boxgrove/boxhome.htm
   Official webpage of the Boxgrove site, a
   Middle Stone Age site located in a stone
   quarry in West Sussex, England, including
   information on its geology, fauna, stone
   tools, and hominids.

The Cave of Chauvet–Pont-D'Arc
www.culture.gouv.fr/culture/arcnat/chauvet/en/index.html
   Official webpage of the Chauvet cave in
   southern France, which contains the world's

first known paintings. Includes information on current research at the site.

The Cave of Lascaux
www.culture.gouv.fr/culture/arcnat/lascaux/en/
Official webpage of the Lascaux site, a complex of caves in southwestern France containing artwork from the Paleolithic period. Includes a virtual tour of the site.

Dmanisi Site
www.dmanisi.org.ge/index.html
Official webpage of the Dmanisi site in eastern Georgia. Includes information on the history and geology of the site, with photographs of the site and fossils found there.

Great Archaeological Sites
www.culture.gouv.fr/culture/arcnat/en/
Sponsored by the French Ministry of Culture and Communication, this website allows the user to navigate to different archaeological sites in France by location or time period and provides links to each site's webpage.

Koobi Fora Research Project
www.kfrp.com
Official webpage of this site in Northern Kenya. Includes information on the history of the site, current research, the fossils (with color images), and associated links.

Krapina Fossil Site
www.krapina.com/neandertals/index_en.htm
This website provides information about the Krapina Neanderthal site in northern Croatia.

Peking Man Site at Zhoukoudian
www.unesco.org/ext/field/beijing/whc/pkm-site.htm
Official webpage of this UNESCO world heritage site in Zhoukoudian, a small village southwest of Beijing.

Sterkfontein Caves
www.sterkfontein-caves.co.za
Official website of the Sterkfontein caves in the province of Gauteng, South Africa, including its history and fossils.

GENETICS

Human Genome Project
www.ornl.gov/sci/techresources/Human_Genome/home.shtml
Official website of the Human Genome Project. Includes information on the project as well as research and teaching aids on genetics.

MendelWeb
www.mendelweb.org
A resource for classical genetics, containing Mendel's papers.

Pubmed
www.ncbi.nlm.nih.gov/entrez/query.fcgi
A text-based search and retrieval system used at the National Center for Biotechnology Information (NCBI), at the National Library of Medicine, this site offers access to articles related to genetics as well as genetic sequence information on a variety of species including humans.

PRIMATOLOGY

PrimateLit Database
primatelit.library.wisc.edu
A bibliographic database of primatology-related articles.

WORKS OF CHARLES DARWIN

The Complete Work of Charles Darwin Online
darwin-online.org.uk
Includes his writings, biographies, and even his autobiography, diary, and field notebooks.

Acknowledgments

It is a privilege to have been invited to participate in a series of books intended for perhaps the most important audience there is. I thank Anand Yang and Bonnie Smith, series editors, for offering me the opportunity to do so, and Nancy Toff, Nancy Hirsch, Martin Coleman, Jane Slusser, and their colleagues at Oxford University Press for shepherding the project along so effectively. At the American Museum of Natural History, Ken Mowbray and Gisselle Garcia were indispensable. This volume is not referenced; but it will, I hope, be obvious to readers that over the years I have benefited from the ideas and insights of many generous colleagues. You know who you are; thank you all.

—Ian Tattersall

Index

Java Man, 93
Peking Man, 93, 125
Homo ergaster. See also Homo erectus
  braincase size, 71
  dating of, 62
  emergence of, 69, 125
  and *Homo erectus*, 64
  toolmaking, 62–63
  Turkana Boy, vii, 60–62
Homo floresiensis, 107
Homo habilis
  dating of, 59
  discovery of, 55–56
  and hominid evolution, 93
  Oldowan industry, 125
  toolmaking, 66
Homo heidelbergensis
  arrival in China, 87
  braincase size, 72
  discovery of, 71
  European fossil record, 73–77, 87, 125
  hominid diaspora, **67**
  and *Homo neanderthalensis*, 82
  language potential, 73
  shelters, **74**, 75
Homo mauritanicus, 68
Homo neanderthalensis
  anatomy of, 78–80, **81**
  appearance of, 125
  burials, 87, 126
  dentition, 85
  diet of, 85–86
  disappearance of, 126
  fossil record of, 27
  Guattari Cave fossil, 27
  Homo antecessor and, 68
  and *Homo erectus*, 64
  and *Homo sapiens*, 82, 85, 94, 103–107
  hunting implements, 77
  Lagar Velho fossils, 79
  language potential, 86
  Little Feldhofer Cave, 78, 84–85
  mitochondrial DNA, 83–85
  radiocarbon dating, 22
  stone tools, 96, 105, **106**, 107
  success of, 83
Homo sapiens. See also Cro-Magnons
  "African Eve," 90–91
  in the Americas, 126
  ancestor with *Homo neanderthalensis*, 85
  "archaic," 87–88, 94
  arrival in Java, 87
  characteristics of, 94
  cognition, 101–102
  emergence of, 55, 88, 94, 99–100, 125
  evolution of, 32–33
  Herto fossil, 94
  Homo antecessor and, 68

and *Homo erectus*, 64
and *Homo floresiensis*, 107
and *Homo neanderthalensis*, 78–80, **81**, 82, 85, 94, 103–107
as hunter-gatherers, 109
language as characteristic, 72–73
mitochondrial DNA, 84, 89–91, **92**
morphology, 95
natural selection, 4
population history, 89–90
radiocarbon dating, 22
skull, 52
and symbolic thought, 101–102
toolmaking, 100
vs. Turkana Boy, 61–621
and urbanization, 122
Y chromosome study, 93
zoological classification, **34**
homozygotes, 15
humans. *See also Homo sapiens*
  bipedalism, 44–45
  braincase size, 38–39
  dentition, 49–50
  evolution of, 35
  language and maturation, 73
  pelvis, **50**
  zoological classification, 32–33, **34**
humerus, definition, 40
hunter-gatherers
  vs. agriculturalists, 121–122
  and evolution, 66
  Homo neanderthalensis, 85–86
  lifestyle, 69
  Magdalenian culture, 108
  Netiv Hagdud, 111
  Paleolithic Era, 109–110
  population growth and, 123
  toolmaking, 76–77
Huxley, Thomas Henry, 78
hyenas, 27, 47, 57–58

Ice Age. *See also* climates
  Aurignacian technology, 96
  extinction of large-bodied animals, 122
  figurines, 98
  Holocene Epoch, 112
  hominid evolution, 87, 90, 93
  Homo heidelbergensis hunting, 74
  Magdalenian culture, 108
India, 37, 120, 126
Indonesia, 107
Indus Valley, 120, 126
inheritance of acquired characteristics, 2–3
interglacial periods, 23, **24**. *See also* climates
Intermediate Stone Age. *See* Mesolithic Era
Iran, 110
Iraq, 110, 112
Iron Age, 115

The
New
Oxford
World
History

Forthcoming Titles